THE KING OF

PRUSSIA COVE

SMUGGLERS OF CORNWALL

BY
JOHN K MARTIN

© Copyright John K Martin 2016
All rights reserved. No part of this publication may be reproduced, distributed, or transmitted in any form or by any means, including photocopying, recording, or other electronic or mechanical methods, without the prior written permission of the publisher, except in the case of brief quotations embodied in critical reviews and certain other non-commercial uses permitted by copyright law.

This book is entirely a work of fiction.
Some of the names are based on real people and real historic events at times but are the work of the author's imagination when required within the story.

Acknowledgment

I would like to thank foremost my family and friends for their help and patience in bringing this book to fruition. I can honestly say that your help and encouragement was most appreciated.

*On Cornish shores a cave is found
No access given
From Craggy Ground*

*Two young Smugglers
Row in from port
Its glowing candles
Light up the fort*

*The cave they enter a forlorn hope
Of booties promise
Not hangman's rope*

*They sip the gin
That helps them cope*

CHAPTER 1

I had worked underground for most of my young life, just as my father, and his father before him had done. As I sit here now an old man; I wonder what would have become of me and my kin if I had stayed in this profession. Thinking back to that sorry old time comes with such clarity. Alas, none of those memories are held dear.

   I remember the rhythmic pounding from scores of picks and hammers, which echoed within the cavernous depths of the mine. We searched for tin. The darkness where we laboured was only broken here and there by a few dull flames of candlelight. I was young then though, and my eyes could pick out the veins of the precious metal with practised ease. Although I detested the long dark hours down that stinking hole, I was particularly good at mining. The idea that we could pluck something valuable from the rock and sell it on to become so many things fascinated me. But that's where my love of mining ended. It was not the fact that the work was back breaking; I have never shied away from hard labour. But I knew then, as I hit the damp rock face with my pick, that I was destined for something far grander, far greater than my miserable existence down the shafts.

On many occasions I would work shoulder to shoulder with my father. It was difficult to get much space to swing, so we would take it in turns. One of us worked the hammer or pick, the other clearing the rubble into buckets. It was then taken to the long chain of carts and pulled to the surface to be sorted from rock to tin.

I will begin my tale on my sixteenth birthday.

A typical day like any other, pounding the rock down the mine. 'What's wrong with you boy?' my father shouted over his shoulder. We had been digging now for hours and sweat poured down his powerful naked back.

'Nothing is wrong; I'm just sick of it today.' In truth I had been sick of it for a long time but would rarely speak my mind in front of my father. Even at sixteen I would not be too old for a thrashing with the strap. He wouldn't do it down the mine though, so I continued my lament further. He turned to me from digging. His face and body were black from muck and soot, which no doubt gave him his terrible cough. All the mine workers got that sooner or later.

'Have you never wished for anything more Pa?' I said quickly before the expected rebuke came. Instead he sighed and wiped his brow with a handkerchief he kept tied around his neck. 'Not this again John. Most men would be thanking God for an honest day's work you know. There are some folk without any employment up there, with empty bellies and no hearth to warm them in the cold of winter.' His patient answer was out of character for him. If I or any of my other brothers complained about our lot, he would normally have flown off the handle into one of his rages. He was a good man, but he'd lived a hard and honest life of toil and frustration. As I stared at him in that moment, I saw what I would become, and knew with a certainty that I would choose a different path.

I let him finish his lecture. 'We Carter's have worked this trade for generations. What else is there for a Cornish man to do?'

I could think of a few things, and perhaps should've held my tongue. I did not wish to aggravate my father any further, but we Carter's were legendary at speaking our minds.

'Well I wouldn't mind owning a mine, instead of slaving down here for pennies.' He smiled at me and shook his head at my naive comment. 'John my boy, you will never own a mine. It takes a small fortune to run one, let alone set one up. But that's not the only reason why.' As he spoke to me, I just wanted to tell him how big my dreams extended. I wanted to yell at him and show him he was wrong. Instead I said frustrated. 'Why?' He put his hand on my shoulder and patiently explained the laws of nature to me. The order of things you might say. 'We don't own the land son. A small few that do, hand down their wealth, legacy and property to their children. They then, if not squandered, pass it down again. I have no land or wealth to leave you boy. All I can give you are the skills to earn an honest living.' I was young and headstrong then. Perhaps I am still stubborn today. This trait would serve me well later. But I think I often infuriated my father with my dreaming. 'There has got to be a better way to make a living than this. Surly a way a man might earn a sum by his wits; instead of sweating blood down here.' The bell rang through the tunnels to signal the end of our day's work. We had laboured to virtual exhaustion, and I yearned to get my head above ground and breathe some fresh air, which had not been pumped down to us.

'I suppose you could go work with your mother's brother hauling fishing nets if you hate this life so much John. But that can be a harder life than you think.' I doubted it could have been much harder than work in the mine. 'Would you ask him father?' We climbed through the tight passage that we'd opened up together over the last few months, and into one of the main passageways that had rails laid down for the ore carts to ride. 'Ask him yourself lad. You may be young, but a Carter does his own dirty work.'

We waited in line to be hauled up to the surface. Down so deep you would not know that in the world above the sun shone over the lush summer meadows of grass. I couldn't wait to get above ground and meet my friends in a tavern and two to quench a thirst I

The King of Prussia Cove

had worked up all day. As we were pulled up on a platform that looked perilously like it was about to break under the weight of yet another heavy load, we began to sing. It was a shanty that was often sung by the men on their way up. My father joined in, his strong baritone voice carried over all others. For such a serious man, he loved to sing. I always used to love hearing his voice belting out as we ascended to the surface.

When we emerged into the early evening air, I spotted a few of my younger brothers sorting the rocks with the women. Mining although a hard occupation, certainly provided work and incomes for the whole family. My mother like me detested it, and mostly stayed at home looking after the many young'uns.

I stopped to talk to one of my younger brothers. He was sifting through the rock merrily and I gave him a wink in greeting. Charles was a very agreeable kind of lad, and I must say, apart from young Harry was my favourite brother.

'Good evening gents; back from your rest down the hole then?' he said cheekily. Unlike me, Charles was quite happy doing anything. When we were much younger he used to follow me around like a lost pup. We used to play war games against other boys from the next village. Those were the days alright; with no thought of hardship on our minds. Our thoughts were full of adventure, and the summers felt endless.

'Enough of that you little bugger. Come on, we're off home,' father said, playfully clipping Charles around the ear. We rounded up the rest of the Carter boys and girls, and began the long walk back to our village, which was a good three miles away. Some of the other men who worked with us lived on the way. We would all walk back together in a big mob, and had some great laughs going home, normally with a detour to a drinking establishment of some description. It was a Saturday, and my birthday. I knew father would drop into the Lion, which was not far from where we lived in Breage. But that night I wanted to meet with some friends, at the livelier Porthleven. The beer houses there were always good for a bit of revelry. He agreed, but said we had to go home first to eat supper with mother and the rest of the family. That was fair enough. I was famished after all.

***

    Our house was on the outskirts of the village. I could see the smoke rise from the chimney in the distance. We were all black and dirty from work, as we were most days. My mother wouldn't let us in the house unwashed and would chastise anyone who dared to do so. Fortunately, there was a well at our place, and someone had set up several buckets of water for us to wash our blackened bodies with. I stripped down to the waste and removed the dirt which was caked on me gratefully. My sisters rolled up their sleeves and washed hands and faces, and quickly hurried into the house to help set up the table. Even from outside, I could smell an aroma that hurried my wash. I could have sworn it was meat of some description, gracing my nostrils. A rare treat indeed for poor people such as we were then.
    Father smelled the meat too. But Instead of rushing in with salivating hunger, he walked into the house after cleansing as solemn as a judge about to don the black cap of execution. I wasn't far behind him. Mother sat at the head of the long oak table expressionless. The table had been a gift to her from her friend's husband, who was a furniture maker from Penzance. My mother was one of those gems in life that made friends and acquaintances wherever she went. My father hated it and looked down at her with a frown I knew all too well. In the centre of the table was a steaming pheasant, the likes of us could not normally afford.
    'Where did that come from Agnes?' my mother just smiled coyly at him. She must have known he would disapprove of her acquisition. 'I got it from Samuel the poacher. Now don't you get on your high horse and lecture me Francis Carter. It's our eldest boy's birthday today, and I wanted him to have a bit of luxury for a change.' That was fine by me, my stomach was grumbling, and the meat was tauntingly juicy. 'I have told you about this before

woman. If someone found out about this, you could go to the clank, or even hang. And all for a poxey bird!'

He was not exaggerating either. The landowners would punish a poacher with utter impunity. It did not matter whether they were a woman, child or grown man. I must say at this point that my family are indeed a God-fearing bunch. But it just never occurred to my mother or to me for that matter, that we would incur God's wrath, just by feeding ourselves the only way we could. On one hand the bird was on our landlord's estate, and therefore his property. But what if the same animal wandered over the border onto someone else's land? Would the ownership change hands from gent to gent? It is a strange crime, and one I hold no fear in breaking.

'If you don't want to eat it, then there is plenty of bread and porridge to eat. I even have a bowl of blackberries here if you find that more palatable,' she said to my father stubbornly. He didn't say another word in argument. It would've been useless anyway, and he knew it.

I began the Lord's Prayer which was taken up by all including mother and father. It was the clearest way to distract them both from bickering. The succulent bird was then eaten quicker than a gull could pluck a kipper from the sea.

My father was the only one who would not partake in the feast. He sat miserably content, picking at a piece of honest bread and oats. Sullenly he left the house to drown his sorrows. He headed to Porthleven, which was a short walk from the farm, and I was not far behind him, and ran to catch him up.

***

He sulked pretty much the whole way to the Ship Inn, where I knew some rascals and friends of mine would already be there. I looked forward to an evening full of merry making and laughter and was not disappointed when I saw my friends who were all in good spirits. My father caught the eye of some of his fellows and made his way to a nearby table where a few gents were playing cards for coppers. I liked a game myself, but I was beckoned over by a good friend of mine named Jack. He handed me a cup of grog, and in no time at all, the stress and hardship from a day of underground labour was washed away. In fact, I could not remember a time when I had laughed so hard after that night.

It was getting late, and the oil lamps were being lit, giving the place a very cosy glow. I was still a bit sore from my days' work and sat down at a table with my friends, where I put my feet up and filled a pipe with tobacco. We smoked, drank and told stories late into the night.

In great haste to seek oblivion, I stumbled to the bar to order another round of gins, when I a noticed a man was yelling at my father. He wasn't much older than me, and by the cut of his cloth, I knew who it was immediately. The Godolphin family were well known landowners of Cornwall for generations. Baron Godolphin owned the mine where we worked, as well as several other tin mines. But it was Francis, his nephew of the same name, who was harassing my father so imperiously. He was a well-known gambling man, and he had been running the mine and making life hard for us all, while he squandered whatever profits he earned at cards.

He was young for such a responsibility but ruled over the desperate workforce with an iron hand. His father before him, the brother of the Baron, was known to be a fair man to the workers. But Francis would not think twice about cutting corners, even when it meant risking the safety of those within his employment. You could say I had taken an instant dislike to the pompous Francis Godolphin. 'Why don't you join a table where the stakes are more suiting to your purse Carter?' I heard him say to my father, who stood from his game, looking embarrassed at the comment. His proud face began to turn red with shame.

One of my friends named Jack could see my intent to step in, and quickly grasped my shirt to stop my intervention. No one else would've stood up to him, for most relied on his favour to work down his shafts. That was why he felt that he could push the likes of us around. 'Stay out of it John, it's not worth it. He's old enough

The King of Prussia Cove

to fight his own battles,' Jack piped up diplomatically. He was usually up for a fight, but he wasn't so drunk to realise that there were just some fights you couldn't win. My father nodded, undoubtedly reigning in his shame and fury, he accepted his place, and left the table without comment. Working in the mine meant his livelihood, and he would not risk it for the sake of pride. 'That's it Carter, off you go, there's a good chap,' said Francis taking his vacant seat. A few more of his rich friends sat down causing an exodus of the poorer card players. They would not be able to afford a single hand at the stakes with which those gents were playing with.

'I'm off home son. Not too late tonight eh, there's church tomorrow, and I don't want you vomiting down the aisles.' I watched him leave with his head down, and his pockets more than likely emptied of coin. I wanted to give Godolphin a good hiding for the insult. I had a bit of a reputation as a fighter, even as young as I was back then. Plugging that swine on the chin however would have been madness, and my father would not have thanked me for it. But there was more than one way to skin a cat. So, I would be patient.

About an hour later a few men came into the tavern with crates of gin and brandy. No one batted an eyelid to the blatant smuggling going on right under their noses. The gents that carried the crates wore fine clothes and expensive but practical leather coats.

We used to pretend to be smugglers ourselves when I was a small boy; and have mock battles along the cliffs and inside the caves. I was a natural leader and due to my size and confidence, I earned the nickname Fredrick, after Frederick the Great, King of Prussia. I had always been fascinated with the Prussian King and admired and aspired to live up to his tactical brilliance. Many people would also comment on my likeness of his portrait, which coincidently hung over the roaring fire where the Godolphin's were playing cards. Just like our silly adventures as young children, I tried to think and scheme about what the great King Frederick would do to these snobs and get away clean. I told my plan to a drunken table of lads, who all rubbed their hands together at the fantasy of getting one back at our supposed overlord. 'That's the way John.' another friend called Samuel said over our table's laughter. He was known locally as Samuel the poacher and was the same man who had supplied my mother with the fine bird for our supper. He was young and foolish, just as I was then. Even so, no one believed I would do anything. They did not realise that I'd been serious in my intent to carry out my scheme and get what little revenge I could for the insult to my father. For that, as well as the many other sleights he had given us over the years.

I was waiting for a distraction; otherwise even my nimble fingers would not be able to pull it off. The opportunity came soon enough, when the innkeeper began to argue with the smuggling lads over the price of their spirits. If that had not happened, then I would have asked Jack to stand on a table and start singing as badly as he did. If that did not distract folks I didn't know what would've. Fortunately, the commotion at the bar was heating up and everyone, including the card players was looking over at the heated exchange.

'I am not paying that price! This is supposed to be free of tax you imbeciles,' I heard the innkeeper shout without a care for who heard him. We all knew where the drink came from anyway. Sometimes a duty-free exchange was even carried out right under the noses of the customs men, who often turned a blind eye to it all. While everyone was watching the commotion, I made my move, and walked over to the Godolphin table, through all the crowds that filled the buzzing tavern. It was always busy in here on a Saturday night, and that was just as well, for when I crept underneath their table, no one noticed me in the slightest. But as I carried out my revenge, I could not ignore the aggressive voices that were still feuding about the price of their wares at the bar.

'Well the price has gone up; take it or leave it. There are plenty of other beer houses we could offload this to,' the smuggler retorted with a thick Irish accent. Under the table, while they argued, I very delicately untied Godolphin's shoelaces. Like the rest of his cloths they were made of the finest material. Most gents in the establishment would've been wearing leather boots that stopped just below their knees. But I had seen his expensive shoes when he had come inside.

Truth be told, I envied him for his wealth. The gentry you see lived by a different set of rules than the common man. If they broke the rules, then they could always buy someone off, or do a deal to get off the hook. But when the likes of us were caught up to no good, then the punishment was usually severe. The trick was to become smarter than the gentry and play them at their own game. With that in mind, I tied his laces on the other foot together, still undetected by anyone. I had to restrain my mirth, which was about to burst out of me and foil my plot before it had been successful. I held my nerve though and tied a double knot for good measure.

I crawled out as silently as a grass snake, and noticed the arguing was over with the smugglers, who were leaving with the cases of gin and brandy they had come to sell. Evidently, they had not come to terms over the price. A thought occurred to me in that instance, but I could not fully grasp it at the time. Before I could think further, my arm was grabbed by one of Francis Godolphin's retainers, a poisonous creature called Arthur Ferris, or Ferris the ferret to everyone else. We often called him that for his rodent like appearance and nature. He was a local man, who served the Godolphin's by attending to their many needs; of which there was many.

He was a footman in a way I suppose and had always been a wretch of a fellow. In social limbo, he was neither one of us, nor one of them, and he was treated with a kind of contempt by all classes. His oily hair, which he'd tried to comb into a similar style as his employer, was pulled into a ponytail by some fancy ribbon, making him look ridiculous.

'Oi, what was you doing under there Carter?' It seemed I was caught, and I rubbed my head as if trying to shake off some kind of fall. 'You know me Arthur; I could never hold my drink. I must have passed out for a minute.' He seemed to believe my story, but he still had a suspicious look in his eyes. He normally did. 'Well clear off; there's gentleman here trying to have a pleasant evening. They don't need the likes of you falling all over em,' he smiled at his own dim wit, exposing uneven ranks of yellow stained teeth. It was beyond my understanding as to why the Godolphin's tolerated the ill-humoured Arthur Ferris. 'Ah, another Carter is it; yes, you are quite right Mr Ferris; on your way lad,' Francis Godolphin said dismissively, not knowing that he may soon be on the floor himself. 'Many apologies sir. It's my birthday today and I am feeling a bit worse for wear. I do beg your pardons.' I graciously bowed and backed away to join my friends, who were all shaking from contained laughter.

I heard Francis make another comment as I backed away. 'Strange Arthur; he actually seemed like he had half a brain. Shame his father is a simpleton.' I could have turned on him for saying that. It took every ounce of my fibre not drag him over the table to show the supposed gentlemen some manners.

As I have said, I was big for my age. The years of digging and working the hammer had made my young body powerful and strong. My shirt bulged from thick muscle, which I carried with an athletic swagger. Most men were wise enough not to antagonise me too much, in fear of my legendary right hook. The rules for the Godolphin's on the other hand were different. They could pretty much talk to us how they wished.

I would enjoy watching the buffoon fall flat on his face. I rejoined my friends who greeted me like a hero, and then we all waited for the pompous brat to get up from his game of cards. Being lazy and spoiled ensured he rarely left his seat much. But even he would have to fill a chamber pot soon enough. Jack was getting nervous and suggested that we go. I told them all to relax and insisted on seeing my handy work completed. Then it happened. He stood and stretched from sitting for too long, draining what was left in his silver tankard. Then as he moved to walk away, the knot I'd tied held fast, and caused him to fall in a great crash. He didn't even have a thought to stop his fall by using his hands to grab hold of a table. Instead he just toppled over like a signpost caught in a high wind.

I had seen enough, and as the place erupted once more with laughter at the expense of poor Francis, we all ducked out of a side door unseen. Oh, how we all enjoyed that little trick. It would later cost my family dear for doing it, but at the time felt like the right thing to do. Was it worth it? I have to say probably no. Sometimes though, I think we are all tempted to be fools.

    We all stumbled home along the coastal path, and I was the King of Prussia in that moment. I accepted my praise as any conquering king should and went over and over the event without tiring of it. 'I can't believe you did it John; and got away with it too. Do you think the ferret will work it out?' chuckled Samuel, who was the only one left with me. Everyone else had broken off in the direction of their homes. 'I don't care what they figure Sam. He was lucky I didn't teach him a proper lesson.' The drunken boast was an empty one, but we were indestructible that night. That was of course until we stopped, and both passed out from way too many brandies.

CHAPTER 2

I awoke to the sound of gulls calling, and a gentle morning summer breeze. The sun was rising steadily, casting the bay in a glorious hue of colour. The scene would have been perfection, if only my head hadn't been pounding so badly from the previous night's adventure. Groggily, Samuel's head popped out of the next hollow. He stretched skywards, and then vomited the contents of his stomach where he knelt. I wasn't so bad, but still reached to my temple, and could have sworn the world was spinning as I gained my feet.

   Suddenly we heard a very loud bang below us on the beach, breaking the peace of the morning's calmness. I looked over the cliff face, and to my astonishment, witnessed what appeared to be a small battle raging. Samuel just looked over at me and vomited again. No one would see us in our little perch up on the cliff tops, but typical to my nature I felt compelled to get closer to see what was happening. 'We should probably get away John,' I heard Samuel whisper to me.

The King of Prussia Cove

I ignored his plea to leave and was glad I did. For below me, there was a about four or five men, shooting pistols at about three others who took shelter behind some rocks which jutted out from the sand. One of the three stood to return fire with a pistol of their own, neatly clipping one of the five in the shoulder. 'Isn't that the Vingoe's down there Sam?' I called back to my very pale looking friend.

The Vingoe family were very well-known and respected smugglers from around Lands' End. Everybody knew John Vingoe, who was steadily loading a pistol to defend himself from the other group. I got on well with his son William, when they showed their faces in the local taverns to sell and sample their cargos of spirits. William was about my age, and like me, was a character of good humour.

Though my head was pounding I could not leave a friend to fight for his life without the help I could most certainly give. 'John you'll be killed if you go down there.' I heard Samuel cry out behind me as I slid down the cliffs natural pathway clumsily. The men attacking my friends were so caught up with the ones shooting at them; they didn't see, nor hear me blundering at them from their flanks. William fortunately saw me sliding down, and he and another fellow they were with ran at the other group with cutlasses in hand. I had no such weapon unfortunately and was only a stone's throw away from them when I started to panic.

All my bravery that I'd felt in that initial moment of lunacy evaporated in an instant. I am ashamed to say now, that I felt a compulsion to turn tail and climb back from where I'd come from. But my reputation would've been in tatters if I had; and so, I charged on with reckless abandon.

I ran as fast as I could, kicking up sand in my haste to reach the fight. Then as I arrived, everything started to move in slow motion. Another shot rang out from William's father John Vingoe, which caught another of our foes in the neck, taking him out of the fight. That evened up the odds nicely, and so we launched at them, three men against three. The only difference was the fact that we were much younger than the foes we faced. As I got closer, I realised the men we would fight were at least a score our seniors, and all with scared and frightful appearances. Incidentally they were the same Irish lads that had argued with the Innkeeper the night before.

  I hit the one closest to me with one of my famously hard right hooks as I ran. I had aimed for his jaw, just as my father had shown me many years ago. He had not seen me coming until it was too late, and collapsed in a heap, unconscious before he even hit the sand. The other two pulled cutlasses and began a vicious fight of cut and thrust with William and his fellow, who appeared to have the upper hand. For someone so young, William was exceptional with his blade, and impressed me greatly, as I watched him dispatch his opponent with only a few clashes of their weapons. The last Irishman who fought against Williams companion, saw the sense to surrender when he realised he was the last man standing, and outnumbered. He'd be hoping to walk away with his life.

  'Please sirs, have mercy on me; I was only going along with what our skipper wanted to do. I beg you, don't kill me.' William's father, John, walked up to the man and without a pause, hit him hard in the face, pulverizing his nose with the pommel of his cutlass. He sank to his knees from the blow, and cradled his broken nose, which was nocked near halfway across his face. John Vingoe then kicked him hard to his head, sending him out cold.

  'Well, if it isn't the King of Prussia himself,' William said to me, breathing hard from the deadly fight. He knew me by my nickname well enough. When his father was doing business in one of our local taverns, William would sometimes accompany him on the voyage, and play with us at our war games. We would always pit ourselves against each other of course. He was the invading pirate after all. He grasped my hand in thanks and pumped it generously. 'Thanks for your help John. For a moment there I thought we were done for. Perfect timing,' he added. His father John came and patted me on the shoulder in thanks also. Samuel the poacher who was somewhat late to our scrap, walked up behind us all meekly, and full of caution. He was another who would not run from a fight, but I did not blame him for his sluggishness when the pistols

The King of Prussia Cove

started firing. He held a couple of stones, and I knew he could throw them just as well as he could shoot a bow or gun. His wicked aim was not needed now however, and I was grateful for being alive and not injured.

To this day, I don't know what compelled me to summon the courage to charge down into that unknown chaos.

But God works in mysterious ways and set me on a path that morning to find my true vocation in life. We all rested on the sand and passed around a flask of brandy to steady our nerves. The men that lay killed or unconscious were not far from where we sat, and I was acutely aware of their presence, as I am sure the Vingoe men were. They did not seem to care much, until one of the Irishmen began to stir.

'We should probably go now lad. This would take some explaining if a customs rider comes along,' John Vingoe announced, looking up at the cliff tops to check whether his worst fears were true. With no more witnesses in sight, he made his way back to his small sloop, which was moored up to some rocks. They kindly offered Samuel and I passage along the coast to my home, and I accepted, considering my headache and reluctance to walk any further. Samuel however did not live very far from where we were, so declined the offer with thanks.

I bid him farewell and would probably see him in church that same day. I told him not to tell a soul about what'd occurred, and he agreed readily. I could trust in Samuel alright to keep a lid on this affray.

As we sailed on a light easterly wind I started conversing with the Vingoe's, who were most grateful of my assistance. It turned out that the Irishmen who had fought against them had held them at gunpoint the day before, near the Lizard peninsular. They'd then relieved the Vingoe's of their small cargo of gin, brandy and about two pounds of tea worth in the region of seventeen shillings all by itself.

I told them what I I'd seen in Porthleven, when the Irish Pirates tried to sell their newly acquired goods to the Innkeeper at the Ship Inn. It'd been pure luck when they spotted the drunken Irishmen where we'd collapsed on the beach. At first light, they ambushed the rogues, and took back their small cargo.

'If there's any way that I can repay you; and it is within my power young John, you have only but to ask.' John Vingoe had said to me while tightening the sail. We picked up a bit of speed and cut through the foaming waves with all the grace of a bird at full flight. The sloop was small; perhaps only 30 tons in weight. But it was perfect for nipping in and out of the coves to land contraband. I reckoned it could have outrun many a vessel from the admiralty or customs, which were often too sluggish and laden with too many men at arms.

I loved the sea and the salty fresh smell from the oceans spray. I loved the sounds, as the waves beat against the boats hull rhythmically. But most of all, I loved the freedom it offered. To be stuck underground for so long had given me an almost insatiable urge to seek open spaces. With that in mind, I knew exactly what favour to ask for. I was nervous to ask him for such a boon but felt I had done them a good service.

'Well since you ask Mr Vingoe, I would very much like to work for you, if you'll pardon my forwardness.' He looked over at his son and they exchanged a look. William nodded slowly, as if vouching for my character. 'Do you know what we do John?' he asked me seriously. I knew alright. I had played games emulating smugglers throughout all my youth. 'I know that you buy goods abroad, and then sell them to folk without the duty paid to the revenue men. I imagine there can be great wealth, in a profession such as that.'

'It's true, it can be rewarding,' he agreed. 'Very rewarding sometimes; but it also carries with it a deadly risk. From pirates and cutthroats, such as the ones we dispatched earlier. We are also hounded mercilessly by his majesty's admiralty, and his many cutters and hulks. Then there are the dreaded customs men, who seek nothing but our demise. They have a hard job in catching us I must confess, but the risk is still great. There's also the feuding between the landowners, who can sometimes be guardian angels,

The King of Prussia Cove

or the devil that condemns us to transportation, and on occasion even the hangman's rope.'

He was putting the frighteners on me, that was clear to see. I understood all the risks involved. Most men of Cornwall did. But that didn't stop everyone partaking in smuggled goods in some fashion. Most people, even magistrates sometimes, turned a blind eye to the common practice. My family for example, lived how my father would say 'in decent poverty.' Yet it was normal for the likes of us to have pots of tea, butter and salt. Brandy, gin and beer were also never far from most families reach. Without paying the extortionate tax, luxurious goods could be bought cheaply, and in modest quantities. A quart of beer in a decent establishment only cost around four pence. I had spent even less than that, getting plastered on gin the night before, for only two pence or so.

'I know the risk sir. Truth be told, my hands are still shaking a bit from this morning's exercise. Although I can't be certain that's not because of last night drunkenness. But to work above ground, would be a novelty for me indeed. Anything would be better than going back down the shafts anymore,' I said honestly. The man that was with the Vingoe's had not said much all morning, but it was he that then said. 'There is nothing wrong with mining lad. My father was a miner and a good one at that.' later on I found out the gent's name was Harry Turner. I liked his calm coolness in the thick of our fight on the beach. He watched and listened more than he spoke, and when he did speak, people listened to him.

'My father is also a miner, and so was my grandfather who died from minor's lung, not so long ago. So, a lot of good it did them for their talent for digging holes. I'm sure I have that same talent, but I would rather seek a more adventurous enterprise sir,' I answered Harry passionately. They all laughed at my little speech, and then I noticed I was nearly at a beach very near my home. John Vingoe gradually calmed his mirth.

'You are more like your mother Agnes,' he said to me, as if he knew her well. I looked at him confused. He would have known my father through his regular outings to the local taverns. My mother on the other hand rarely left the small farm where we lived.

'How do you know my mother sir?' He started smoking a pipe, while the other two men swung the sloop towards the shore. 'I've sold your mother goods for years now. Don't tell your father mind you; I don't think he would like it. I don't think he would like you working for me neither,' he told me cautiously. It was true that my father would hate the fact that I would earn my keep in such a fashion. But my father had also told me to do my own dirty work, if I wanted to find alternative employment. He had said that he was happy for me to go fishing with my uncle. So, I was doing my own dirty work, by making a living on the sea.

'I have already expressed my desire to him Mr Vingoe. He would probably want me to live and die like the rest of our family. Like him.'

'But I won't live out my life like that,' I added. We pulled into waters shallow enough, so I could get out of the sloop about knee deep. As I climbed over he took my hand and thanked me again for my help in the fight against the Irish.

'I always repay a debt young John Carter. I like the cut of your jib, and the way in which you have conducted yourself this morning. As you are so eager, I do have the perfect job for someone like yourself. I need someone to distribute for me, if you would be interested of course? I need someone to sell my goods around the villages, all about this area. How does that sound?'

It sounded fine to me. I knew most of the folks who lived along the coast. I also liked dealing with people, and had gained many a friend, both young and old for my agreeable nature. It was a step in the right direction any way. 'I accept sir,' is all I said 'good,' he replied, and threw me a package which looked like cheese. 'That's for your mother.' I thanked him and was told to meet him at the same spot in one week's time, on the following Saturday to collect my first shipment of contraband to sell.

My head was still spinning, and I left for home to meet the consequences of staying out all night. My mother would've been amused by my tale. But I knew my father would have taken to a dark mood because of my actions.

The King of Prussia Cove

***

The walk home was short, and the sun was now completely up and on my back. I journeyed uphill, getting further away from the sea, eventually reaching the outskirts of our little farm. We had a few chickens that produced eggs for the family. Sometimes we would sell any surplus eggs to locals, when times were hard. Times in those days always seemed hard. No matter how hard we all worked, our lives just stayed the same. Decent poverty may have been good enough for my father, but I, like most of my brothers, would eventually seek more.

The cockerels screamed a challenge as I passed, and Charles stepped out of the farm house, checking on the commotion. Upon seeing me, he ran over to tell me that my father was in a frightful temper. 'What happened last night John? Pa came home late and has been sulking all morning. I'll warrant he won't be pleased with you turning up at this hour.' My younger brother Harry came over to where we stood. I hid behind a wall from him, and he rushed over to see me. At five years old, Harry loved it when I jumped out on him and pretended to be a monster. He had a full head of thick curly dark hair. A beautiful boy. I jumped out as he approached and was rewarded with a screech of feigned terror. 'Where you been King John?' He loved calling me king, and always looked up to me as a kind of hero. They all did to a certain extent, but I was soft on Harry, for his character was as big as my own.

'I've been out to sea fighting monsters of the deep. Look at my shirt lad; you can see some of its blood where I chopped it to pieces.' The monster's blood was where I had been sick all down my shirt. It was my clean shirt which I normally wore for church. When I made some serious money from smuggling, I would be sure to purchase some more clothes. Finer clothes than I had now. The shirt I wore down the mine was as black as the hole we worked in. I would hope to never wear that rag ever again. 'Is that true John?' said little Harry mystified by my outlandish claim of being a monster slayer. I winked at him and ruffled his hair affectionately. Then I heard my father shout out from the doorway of the house.

'What time do you call this John Carter? Don't think because it was your birthday last night, you can do as you please around here.' I put my head down sheepish at the thought of telling him of my job opportunity. As he stood scalding at me my mother came out with a basket to collect some eggs. I was hungry and could have eaten a cow. The eggs would do nicely though; especially if there was any bread left over. I threw the packet of cheese at my mother, who smelled it and asked. 'Where did you get this from?'

'It's a long story,' I replied evasively.

Later that day, when Charles and I were alone, I told him most of what had happened. He looked at me after that in even more awe than he already had. The story I told my mother and father however was much less interesting. I told them that I'd passed out with Samuel by the sea, which was true. I left out the part where we fought the Irish Pirates, and nearly being killed for our efforts.

I told them that I met the Vingoe lads resting from a nights fishing, and that I had asked John Vingoe for a job distributing his goods to the locality. 'I take it that the packet of cheese came from John Vingoe?' I could see where his question was leading. 'Yes.' I replied.

'Are they fishing for cheese now then?' I wanted to answer the sarcastic question with one of my own. Instead I went down the avenue of reason. 'I helped him out this morning, that's why I'm late. He didn't have any coin to pay me with, so he gave me the cheese with thanks. I know he smuggles a bit, but I want to work for him. I'm a man now, you've said so yourself Pa.'

'He's right Francis; if he wants to work for the Vingoe's, then he should,' my mother said helpfully. She was a remarkable woman, my mother. For someone who'd worked so hard around the farm, as well as looking after my brothers and sisters, she was still the prettiest and smartest women around. I would be lucky to meet a woman as strong, and kind as my mother.

'What about your job at the mine. You're just going to walk away from a regular wage, to go off into the unknown?'

The King of Prussia Cove

All my after could see was a looming abyss. I Just didn't see it that way, but they both knew I wouldn't budge from my position. We argued for another ten minutes or so, when finally, my father agreed reluctantly not to stand in my way. 'Very well son!' He said. 'But if you can't earn a wage equal to what you received at the mine. Then you must beg the owners to take you back. They would too with your strong arm.'

So, it was agreed.

It amazed me just how quickly my fortunes had turned overnight. One minute I was lamenting over my sorry existence; to then be given an opportunity to live my dreams. I praised God mightily that day in church. He had blessed me and put opportunity in my path. I believe he still watches over me, and I try to repay him, by dealing with my fellow man with the utmost honesty. People would know and trust the name Carter.

I wanted all the folk of Cornwall, and abroad to know my name. The following week would be the beginning. But as I sat in prayer in our Methodist Church, I knew that God was helping me to realise my dreams - Dreams which were as big as the whole world.

CHAPTER 3

I had not gone to the mine on the following Monday, and that was just as well. Francis Godolphin had been humiliated by my actions, and he knew it was me who'd tied his laces. He knew it, because Arthur the ferret Ferris had whispered into his ear, that it was I who'd been skulking under their table. He would not have the satisfaction of ending my employment though. For on the next day, I made my way there, so I could tell him in person that I no longer wished to serve down his mine. To my relief I was glad to find out that he was not there. The shame and ridicule from the other lads was just too much for him to tolerate, and he couldn't very well dismiss his whole workforce. He left the Ferret there instead to give everyone a hard time.

'Carter, I want a word with you,' he said to me, and spat a gob of tobacco before my feet. 'If you think you've got away with your little stunt the other night, you're wrong. Mr Godolphin wants you gone sir. There is no more work for you here.' I pretended I was mortified by his judgment. Because it dawned on me that he would not only punish me for my actions, but also my whole family. It

The King of Prussia Cove

turned out that my fears were to be proven true. He did keep them on at the mine; yet in spite of me, he made their lives a living hell. He deducted pay in the form of fines from all of them. Even the Carter children, who sorted the ore as it came to the surface, were penalised for my actions.

Later when I became more successful, most of my family came and worked with me. At the time however, life was very hard for us.

We were tenants on Lord Arundell's land, which was substantial. Since the thirteenth century, the Arundell's had held great swaths of the land in Cornwall. Most of which was around the coast, where they enjoyed salvaging rights from any wrecks, or valuable flotsam fortunate enough to wash ashore.

The other wealthy families who held considerable areas of land were the Bassets, the St Aubyns and the Onslow-Borlace family.

There were other landowners of course; notably the Duchy of Cornwall and the Godolphin's. But apart from the Godolphin's; our lives were mainly in the hands of Lord John Arundell and his many agents.

He was a fair landlord and had a reputation for looking after his tenants. He was also fiercely territorial, concerning any claim made on a wreck which he deemed ownership of. In those days, it was a common occurrence to be in dispute with many of the other wealthy landowners over a wreck or flotsam claim. Most disputes were conducted in a gentlemanly kind of order.

The feuding between the Arundell's and the Onslow-Borlace's was the exception to that. There was much jealousy from the gentry towards the Arundell's, who claimed wrecking rights even into other landowner's territory. They could do this because of an old Royal decree which granted them salvage, upon anything abandoned at sea, as far as a man could see a barrel of ale on a clear day. Even if they sold land to another family over the centuries, they still would hold claim to wrecks or other valuables because of that old royal decree.

At times, violence between the two families would ensue, like the occasion when a ship was wrecked off the coast, near the Borlace land at Lanisly.

George Borlace the younger had claimed rights to a wreck, and had sent salvagers to dismantle the mast, which he kept in a back yard at his estate. But Lady Arundell had heard about the wreck also. Their reach and purses, employed the eyes of many folk who'd be rewarded handsomely for reporting news of this sort to them. So, she sent her bailiff John Treluddra to make the families claim. But George Borlace had also employed men of worth, who threatened to beat poor old John Treluddra with clubs to with an inch of his life. Upon his return, Lady Arundell was furious at what had happened to her agent, and eventually fought the case legally through the courts.

In the end the families claim was indisputable, due to their historical paperwork which was signed by the king himself.

George Borlace was found guilty and fined for his actions. I never understood why. But when the gentry broke the law, the punishment was usually a fine. However, when the likes of us; the common man was caught doing much the same thing, it could have meant a time in prison, transportation or even the death penalty.

This was one of the reasons why I and other folk like me in Cornwall, could see no wrong in smuggling and wrecking. If it was good enough for our lords and masters, then it was ethically good enough for us. We on the other hand had to be careful that we were never caught, and the best way of that not happening, was by making friends in the highest, and the lowest of places.

Like a rope holding a sail taught; success in the smuggling business was only as strong as its weakest knot. If someone informed on my activities from the poorer classes for instance, then I was finished. But if I fell out of favour with the Lord of the land, or other important members of the gentry, then I would also be ruined. It would be their support and influence in later years that ensured I kept my liberty, as well as my freedom to operate unhindered.

I was only just beginning my journey to greatness, and like a wee whippersnapper, I would have to fight for a place in this world and earn my reputation.

***

It was another clear morning, and the sun looked to be coming up within another hour or two. The dark sky was already turning on the eastern horizon, as I gazed out over the sea, waiting for my first batch of contraband to sell.

A day's work in the mine used to fill my thoughts with dread for what the day would bring. I would always find it hard to sleep knowing what toil to expect.

My first day smuggling in contrast was the complete opposite. I had awoken early, excited about all the adventures I would have, and I imagined how much money I would make, and the fine cloths I would wear.

Most people, especially in the mining community, topped up their pay by selling what they could get their hands on through wrecks or smuggling.

My family also made a little extra by selling what we could produce on the farm we rented. Smuggling for me would now become my full-time occupation. So, I had to start looking at it as my new profession, instead of earning bits and pieces on the side.

I would of course always look to other avenues of income; such was my enterprising nature. But without the safety net of a regular wage, I had forced my hand into providing for myself, and finding my own money and wealth.

I remember laying on the sand on a warm star lit morning, waiting and watching, hoping that the Vingoes would turn up for our arranged meeting. A trickle of disappointment washed over me as I considered the very likely fact that they may not make it. My worrying was short lived, when I spotted a sloop coming from the west, just as the sun was beginning to come up on the horizon. I could still see the brightest of stars, but there was enough light to navigate the treacherous coastline. The Vingoe lads just happened to be masters at this kind of sailing.

I hurried down to meet them on the beach. They wouldn't want to linger too long and unloaded their cargo of about ten crates of spirits as quickly as physically possible. The goods were taken to a nearby cave, and hid cunningly in a carefully cut nook, high up within. It was a marvellously clever hiding place, and unless you knew where to look, you'd have completely missed the crates of duty free goods stored inside its dark depths.

'We store it up here on the shelves we've cut for many reasons John. The most obvious reason is so no passer-by, including the customs men, will find it in plain sight. It also helps that at high tide; the cave becomes virtually inaccessible, but remains nice and dry where we store it,' John Vingo informed me, as we unloaded the sloop. William and I had done all the lugging, as he explained the ins and outs, of how his small operation worked.

I had received a bit of schooling when I was very young but felt compelled early on to earn my keep and help the family survive and prosper. My real education though was just beginning. I was learning from the very best about how to become a smuggler.

'Of course, we also have to hide our goods from other smugglers who use the caves up and down this country. That includes pirates, like the ones we fought off last week, and even some of the admiralty. They're at it just as much as we are you know.'

While talking to me he wrote down everything which he'd unloaded on a piece of paper and handed it over to me. 'Can you write?' he asked.

'I can get by,' I told him truthfully. He seemed impressed that I could. Most folk of our ilk couldn't you see.

We were encouraged to learn how to read the Bible at church, so we could learn about Gods glory from the pages of the good book.

It was John Wesley who'd spoken in our churches and expanded the Methodist movement to the far reaches of Cornwall. I must confess that I enjoyed his impassioned sermons when he preached about Satan tempting us away from God's light.

I agreed with him on the most part. But his ethics were sometimes floored when it came to smuggle for instance. The man hated it and would write letters to London cursing the likes of us for our wicked ways. Later in life his views would soften, and I would count him as one of my friends. But if I told him what I'd been up to on the beach that morning, he would have damned me where I stood.

'When you sell an item; mark down just how much you've sold it for, next to where I've written. On the other side, I've made a note explaining the minimum amount you need to take for everything. That will be my cut of the bargain. Anything you can make on top belongs to you. Fair enough eh young Carter?'

It sounded more than fair. For what he wanted for gin and brandy, I knew I could get so much more than that. I supposed without men like me however, he would've had to have distributed it all himself. That of course would take up precious time for a man like him; time spent where he could've been purchasing more goods from Guernsey.

I had a great deal to learn from him, but already understood the basics enough to feel confident in selling for the Vingoes.

'How long have I got to get rid of it, before you get back sir?' I asked him when we left the cave.

'I will be back in two weeks; but don't worry if you can't sell it all by then. It'll probably take a few months to clear this amount for a new lad. Some of my top distributors could do it in a fortnight or so, once they make the right connections. I'll be back then to see how you're doing. You'll be fine though, I know talent when I see's it.'

He had placed a lot of trust in me for leaving such valuable goods in my care. I could have taken the lot and done a runner for all he knew. But I guessed that his son William would've spoken well for me. He told me later that any man who would risk his life to help a friend as I did, was alright in his book, and so I could be trusted with a few cases of contraband.

***

With a new purpose, and a plan forming on how I would distribute the goods, I made my way inland and back to the farm. My father, along with most of my family, had gone to work at the mine. The only folk at home were my mother, and the children too small to work. It was a real novelty being above ground for a change, and I kicked my boots off happily. Mother was chopping some potatoes and carrots for supper, and as she worked, I tried to find out how she knew John Vingoe.

I told her the truth about my new line of work, to which she smiled knowingly, stopping what she was doing.

'You think I don't know what old John Vingoe gets up to? Well, if we are being truthful, I will tell you some secrets master Carter.' It was supposed to have been my confession to her, not the other way around.

My face must have told her that I was surprised, so she explained her meaning by taking me to one of the many outbuildings used by the chickens when it became cold. She brushed off some straw on the floor revealing a slab of stone in the corner. Carefully, she slid it to one side, revealing jars of tea leaves, and a few bottles of gin. She took out a tin which held some pepper also. Pepper had risen again in tax, and a good profit could be made if you got your hands on the duty-free kind. King George's purse was fat enough I reckoned, so he wouldn't miss what we kept from him.

'My word; I had no idea!' I said flabbergasted.

I knew she bought the odd thing or two from Samuel the poacher. But this was something I had thought beyond my mother, and I told her as much.

'How have you hidden this from Pa and the others? How have you hidden this from me?' I said laughing with her. She reached over to loosen another stone on the ground, and pulled out a purse of coin, with some notes. It was about four pounds in total.

'I've squirrelled this away for a rainy day. Don't tell your father about it John. Remember, I know you're a smuggler. You keep my secret and I'll keep yours,' she said to me in a hushed voice.

'I won't say a word. I'd be a hypocrite if I did, wouldn't I.'

'Yes, you would.'

She put everything away the way it'd been and swept some straw back over the stone. 'This is a good place to hide things John. Your father doesn't come in here much, so you're welcome to use it as you please.'

I now understood that I did in fact take after my mother after all. She had managed to keep her dealings a secret for all those years. My admiration for her went up even more than it already had been.

Don't get me wrong, I looked up to my father in many other ways. He was a hard worker, and a good man. But those qualities alone would not bring a person wealth and prosperity. You never saw any of the gentry for example breaking their backs for a shilling.

After showing me her stash, my mother helped me to get started on my endeavour. I did have an idea of my own on how to proceed, but her advice proved to be invaluable.

We discussed my distribution strategy for a few hours until about lunchtime. She gave me some great advice about where to go, and where to sell my goods.

So off I went to start doing it, and my great adventure was about to begin

CHAPTER 4

Mr Vingoe had told me that I would have been lucky to get rid of the modest amount of goods he'd given me. He was returning in two weeks, and I went straight to work to prove to him I could clear the lot within the fortnight given. I visited all the local beer houses and Inns within a day's walk. I was known to some of the people already, and that helped speed things up very nicely.

I was a new face however in my new line of work and had to portray myself as a respectable dealer of goods; irrespective of where it came from. I knew just how to talk to people, and in no time, I was selling.

I was doing very well with the locals within easy reach of our farm; but I needed to sell more in the lager towns like Helston and Penzance.

So, one morning I got up early, and made the long walk to Helston, with utter confidence I would succeed. I carried as much gin and brandy as I could, but because the tea would fetch a higher price, and was extremely light, I took it all with me. This turned out to be wise a decision, as on my way into town I stopped off at

The King of Prussia Cove

as many homesteads as I could, trying to sell. My strategy and easy selling manor was so good I have to say, that by the time I got to Helston, I had very near nothing left of what I had brought with me.

That didn't stop me making a few sales on a promise though.

Selling for me came as easy as breathing. I knew my numbers well and had a quick understanding of how much I could get for each item. People would always relieve a smuggler of their wares. The tax placed on such luxuries made them affordable when sold without the heavy duty owed.

But I was not the only person selling such contraband, and nearly came to blows with a well-known smuggler in town, when I was trying to sell to an interested innkeeper.

'Who do you think you are, coming here and taking my customers?' he said aggressively?

I probably should've shown more fear, for a youngster as I was. But I have always been good at reasoning and negotiating with people. So Instead of challenging a much older and experienced smuggler, I offered an apology for not seeking him out beforehand. 'I'm distributing for John Vingoe; sorry if I have caused offence sir,' I said diplomatically.

He softened to that comment but was still sore because of the fact he had a new competitor, even if I was so young. I could understand his grievances; I on the other hand hadn't worn out the soles of my boots to get here, to be beaten at my first challenge. 'I'm here to stay sir, and don't wish to fight a good fellow such as yourself,' I said to him as agreeably as I could. An idea to solve this problem formed in my mind, and I added quickly. 'We could help each other out you know. You can buy the rest of my goods off me. I'll even come down in price as low as I can. Then you can then sell it off to your regulars and make a very tidy profit, without sailing out to sea.' He looked interested, yet still not convinced.

'I already have a supplier, and your prices would have to be low indeed for me to buy anything.'

He then told me he had a small sloop that he sometimes sailed over to Guernsey to purchase his goods.

'That's all very well and good, but the quantities I can get hold of are considerable. I would also be taking away your risk at sea from the customs men,' I added.

He nodded encouragingly; but there was still the issue of my credentials. I was so young and unknown in the smuggling circles after all.

I hated lying, but in that moment, I decided to tell a little fib which was relatively close to the truth. 'It is true sir; I am young. But I've been working with the Vingoe's for a while now and know my business. This is why he has placed so much trust in me to distribute on his behalf.'

That little fib in the end was enough for my first smuggling contact. We set out price terms and shook on our deal. His name was James Thomas and had originated from Wales. His father like mine was a miner and had come to Cornwall on a promise of work and prosperity. James like me had not desired to walk the path of his parents and had taken to smuggling for the last five years or so. He was earning a good living out of it too, even before I came along. He told me later that he could sense that I would go far, and gave me a chance because of my charming arguments, as well as a good price I offered.

So, in less than a week, I had sold the whole amount of goods which I'd been given. A feat I would soon learn was impressive indeed for a veteran, let alone a mere novice as I was then.

I had promised James more contraband and took it to him the next day.

Maybe I had promised too much. In no time at all, I was left without any of the spirits to my name after our agreement. I just hoped that old John Vingoe would have some more for me to sell soon.

***

In the meantime, I waited for the Vingoe's to return, and counted all the money I had made. After deducting what I owed my supplier, I realised the profits were extraordinary.

I had to count it several times over to make sure I had not made some mistake. I kept shaking my head in amazement at the amount of money now in my possession. It was so good, that I had earned more smuggling in a fortnight, than I could in about six months' down that dirty old mine.

The madness of it all was that my hands were clean, and I had been breathing fresh clean air while I earned this small fortune. It was a fortune to me then too.

I hid the money away, along with my mother's small stash, and waited for Mr Vingoe with great anticipation. Over the next week, I busied myself by making more and more contacts locally, and introduced myself to folks who I'd never acquainted myself with before.

Eventually the two weeks passed, and once again I waited for the arrival of the Vingoe boat. The sea was a bit choppier than it'd been the last time.

I caught sight of the sloop and watched it sail into shore on a stiff westerly wind. I couldn't hide my pride when they disembarked and grinned like a cat that got the cream.

'Well lad; how did you do?' Mr Vingoe senior asked me expectantly. I shook their hands before I answered. 'I've done alright I reckon sir,' I boasted. 'We've brought more cargo if you need a top up.' It was plain to tell that I had sold a decent amount. My happiness was evident.

'I'm glad you have more, for I will need it,' I said cockily

'Oh really; I think he's done just as well as you said he would William.' He smiled at his father and then at me. 'Well come on then; how much did you sell you rascal?' William prodded.

'All of it!' I said.

'All of it?' they both said in unison.

'Yes, all of it! I must declare I've enjoyed every minute.' I held out a purse with their money, minus what I had earned. I had put in a few extra shillings as a way of thanks for giving me my start. I hoped it would sweeten any future business they could give me too. 'My goodness John Carter, even our best lads couldn't get rid of that amount in two weeks.'

'One week, Mr Vingoe. It was all gone by one,' I said smirking. I could tell he didn't believe me, but he did give me the chance to see how well I could do with another batch. 'I am impressed Master Carter, and that doesn't happen often I can tell you. It just so happens I have a slightly larger amount than before on the boat. Do you think you can do it again in such time?'

He was clearly testing me, and I loved it. I felt like I could have moved mountains or travelled to the moon and back in that moment. 'I can sir. In fact, I think I can move much more if you can supply it.' Maybe I was being too big for my own boots, as I tried to become great too quickly. But I was in a rush to become successful, a man of means. I'd wasted too much time down the mine already and was eager to prove my worth. I didn't tell them on that day about my contact in Helston. They were both honourable men, but I didn't want them cutting me out so early on; so, I stayed quiet about it.

'I can get you more. Much more if you can move it. Let's see first if you can do it again in a week. If you can, I'll send William up here every week. Any more than that and we'll have to use a different place to land. The customs men aren't all as stupid as they look you know.'

I'd been so caught up in my own magnificence that I had not even thought about the customs men. I would have to use more caution I then decided. It had been so casual to sell the goods that it never occurred to me that it was a crime. The risk of getting caught however was high, and they would pounce on an unsuspecting smuggler quicker than a hawk can scoop up an unsuspecting mouse. I promised myself that I would not get sloppy. We discussed that topic in great length before they left me with another cave full of goods to sell.

The cave was brimming once again, and all stored on the manmade shelf high up. Unfortunately, every time I needed to gather anything from the shelves, I had to climb up the slippery rock.

Instead of risking any bottles of spirits being broken, or more importantly causing myself a mischief, I needed to come up with a way of getting up onto the shelf quickly and safely. Climbing the seaweed covered rock up and down would have been fun, until one of my barrels or bottles was dashed, along with my earnings.

Walking up the beach, I came across a piece of driftwood which had washed into shore a fair while ago. It looked about as high as the shelf inside the cave and had many thick branches all the way up its trunk. I used it like a ladder, and I could rest the heavy barrels on the way up and on the way down. We had used a length of old rope before, so my new crude ladder was a marked improvement. The only downside was the fact that the driftwood had to be moved in and out of the cave. Or someone would have guessed that there was something worthwhile at the top of the climb. Although heavy, the strength gained from working underground for so long had paid dividends.

Nothing but profit had been on my mind. That was until I had my first scare, with what all smugglers hated and feared the most.

The customs men!

I rushed to take my driftwood ladder from outside of the cave, and brushed the sand clean of footprints, from my morning's work. I neared the caves entrance to peep out and gain a better look, and noticed a large Cutter, sailing across the cove. It was not massive, like some of the other large hulks that stalked the coast. Maybe it was about one hundred and thirty tons or so, maybe much less. I didn't hang around long to find out, as I eased back into the caves darkness, hoping I had not been seen. My heart beat hard inside my chest when I realised the Cutter had weighed anchor not far from where I hid.

So many terrible feelings came over me; mainly terror. I imagined that someone had informed on me after I had blabbed about being the new big man in town. It had felt as if I'd been inside the cave for hours. Every now and then, I would crawl to the mouth, and see if the dreaded customs men had found me. To my good fortune on that occasion, they left about lunch time and I could go about my day without being taken or killed. Being killed was a real threat in the profession too. There were always tales of battles, and scraps with the customs men, and violence would often be a consequence of an encounter.

It was getting late in the day to make the walk to Helston, so I walked to another farm where I had sold some tea the week before. This farmer was in the dairy business, and had many cows that produced milk, cheese and beef for the tables of the wealthy. It was a noticeable difference in comparison to our little farm. We paid our landlord just over two pounds a year to rent the small piece of land. We grew just enough to feed ourselves and sold what was left for extra money. We kept some chickens and enjoyed a kind of decent poverty, as my father called it many times.

This farm however was very large indeed, and it was a joy to take in the lush green landscape around me. There had been the perfect balance of rain and sun that year, making growing conditions excellent. The farmer came out to greet me, with dirt on his hands and sweat on his brow. He had no doubt worked since the sun came up, perhaps even before that. He would have an almighty thirst after a day's labour on the farm.

I caught the whiff of cow dung as he neared me. It was all over his boots and was starting to harden in the heat of the day. The beer that I carried must have seemed like a gift from God.

'Oh, my goodness, you have outdone yourself lad. Give that here,' he said, snatching the skin of ale I had offered him. I didn't mind. He would be good for payment. I knew him from church and he was an honest Methodist and a gentleman.

Most people in Cornwall, nay even the whole country looked upon the smuggled goods as a necessary evil. How else was the impoverished going to get any pleasure out of life? The farmer drained about a third of the beer, and I laughed at his urgency to get it down his neck. He wiped his mouth with his shirtsleeve, and we made a deal on the beer he had near finished before I'd left.

'I was wondering if I could ask a favour of you Mr Avery,' I asked him innocently. There had been more than one reason to come here than selling goods after all. The last load that the Vingoe's had left me was much bulkier than before. I had a few barrels of ale back at the cave, in addition to the jars and bottles of the other contraband. I asked them at the time how I would move such a weight, and he told me that I should think of something. This was probably another test, to see if my boasts would prove true a second time. I would not disappoint him

'A favour you say… If I can grant it, then you may ask young Carter,' he said cheerfully with the effects of drinking too quickly lightening his mood.

'Well I have more cargo to move sir and need a horse and cart to get it up to town. I would like both if you could spare them for a day or two.'

He rubbed his stubbly chin and thought about my request briefly.

'I'll tell you what; you leave me another skin of beer, and you can borrow a horse and cart for a week.' That was generous indeed, and I shook on it before he changed his mind. I thanked him, and the next day I led the powerful looking working horse and cart to the beach where my little cave was. When I came up with the idea of moving the goods in this way I was mightily pleased with myself for thinking of it. Now with the cart packed and well on my way to town, I realised what a blunder I had made.

Cornwall was a beautiful country, of hills and rocky formations. Its people were natives and had fought as Britons, against the Romans, Saxons and Vikings. All foes throughout history had feared the Cornishman; for he was not only fierce but had an intimate knowledge of his land. They would use this knowledge to their advantage. Something I should have thought about when leading my goods to Helston.

Cornwall you see, hardly had any roads. There was talk of extending the main road all the way to Marazion, but that had met with much resistance from the locals strangely. You would have thought that commerce and ease of travel would outweigh the desire to be isolated. The isolation however, made it easy to smuggle goods in and out of the county, as well as hide it from the crown. It made a smuggling man's life that much easier because of the lack of roads.

But it was slow going to Helston and took me most of the day to get there, where I met up with James Thomas again.

CHAPTER 5

The streets were clear of people when I arrived; John Wesley was preaching in the town's Methodist church and had drawn a great deal of folk to hear him speak. I found Thomas at an inn by the harbour, drinking with a few men. He spotted me as soon as I came in and shook my hand in greeting.

'So, do you have more for me then?' he asked expectantly.

'I've got a cart load outside. I nearly broke the poor horse's back trying to get it here.' He winked at me and nodded over to the innkeeper, who disappeared down a cellar.

'We need to be quick and get it all inside John. I think there's a duty man in church today,' he warned with a slight tone of urgency. It took us no time at all to get the contraband out of sight and down the cellar. The lads James had been drinking with lent a hand, which I was grateful for. A few men who were sitting in the corner of the Inn faced the wall as we worked, so if he was questioned, they could swear honestly that they hadn't seen us. That was common in those days, and it always looked so strange when we unloaded, to see folks, all with their backs turned from us.

Once we unloaded the cart, James bought a round of drinks for everyone. He was young like I was then, as were his friends who were all in their early twenties and didn't have a care in the world. None had families that depended on them, and we sat around for an hour or so, trading stories and drinking heavily.

James thanked me greatly for making good on my word.

'To be honest, I thought you were full of delirium when you told me what you had.' He slid over a bag of coins, which disappeared into my pocket.

'I need a better way of getting here from where I live,' I said miserably. He was amused that I had not thought of the obvious solution. After a bit of teasing, he finally gave me a piece of advice. I should have thought of it myself it was so simple. 'Why don't you bring it here by boat you fool?' He laughed, and I just stared at him dumbly, thinking what an idiot I had been.

Normally I prided myself on my intelligence and ingenuity. But it had not even occurred to me to bring it here by sea. 'I can't afford a boat yet,' I said trying to cover my stupidity.

'A small dingy isn't that much John. You can use mine if you want.' We had only met twice, but James and I hit it off straight away. It was like we had known each other for years; when in fact, we knew very little of each other.

My judge of character has rarely failed me, and James was a character indeed.

I accepted the use of his small boat and started moving our meagre cargoes up and down the coast. He taught me the basics of what he knew about sailing and the sea in general. Eventually we were intimate with every nook and cranny, and started finding more caves to store our goods in. Our friendship and his dingy had made transportation so much easier for us, that our profits grew and grew.

One night, as we camped out on the beach, I asked him something that had been on my mind for a few days. 'I've been thinking James.' I said to him, as he was cooking a fish over the fire and trying not to burn his fingers. 'Thinking eh... I'd be careful I was you John.' He yelped suddenly as the flames scalded his hand comically. 'I was thinking that we should go into business together.' He laid the charred fish down on a rock and shook the pain away from the minor burn.

'Business is good at the moment; I must admit that. What do you propose?'

I had saved up enough money to buy a bigger boat and sail to Guernsey to buy gin. By doing that, we could earn extra by removing the Vingoe cut. I had worked for the Vingoe family for months now, and they were very happy in how things were working out. I would still take their goods for distribution. It was too lucrative not to; plus, I felt like I had owed them for giving me a start. I had discussed my venture with John Vingoe before I approached James. He was happy for me to do my own thing on the side. He even had the perfect little sloop for me to buy and said I could sail over to Guernsey with him, so he could show me its coast line, and where to go.

Everyone in life, young lads more so, need a role model and a mentor. John Vingoe was that for me. He taught me about navigation and tides. He showed me the many places where to buy from, and the places where not to. It was a smugglers apprenticeship in a way; and I took to it like a fish to water. I spoke to James that night on the beach about my vision to expand as much and as fast as I could. We were making a handsome living just as we were. But my dreams were not going to come true with comfort and contentment.

'I would never have thought someone as young as you could pull it off John. But I was impressed the moment we met. So, I suppose I'm with you,' James decided, accepting my offer of partnership. His voice was deep and resonating and still had a twang of welsh to his accent. He was slightly taller than me, and I was tall for my age. He was thicker set though and carried himself with a swagger of confidence. He would be a handful, if there was anyone foolish enough to mess with him. If I hadn't crossed his path, he would've carried on smuggling in his town of Helston, in blissful ignorance of the greatness he could've achieved.

***

Over the next few months, the days grew shorter and the nights became long. We jointly purchased the sloop from Mr Vingoe on credit, with a promise to pay for it outright later. It was called the snapper. A silly name, but it was unlucky to change it to something else, so it stayed.

William joined us many times on our trips to Guernsey. One day at the start of December, he told me why his father had helped me so much.

'He couldn't believe it when you charged into a bunch of big pirates to help us. We owe you our lives King John,' William confessed while steering the boat.

'Steady on; I was only doing what any good Christian would do for a friend,' I told him, trying to stay as humble as I could. Maybe he wouldn't hold me in such high regard if he knew how terrified I was.

'No. What you did was braver than any man he'd seen; and he has been in a few scraps I can tell you. He couldn't believe how quickly you turned your hand to smuggling too. You're a natural.'

I had thought about that day on the sand, fighting the Irish pirates many times in my life. I would have plenty more fights after that; too many for my liking. But that fight was the day God had guided me to what I was meant to do.

***

By the time Christmas came around, I decided to splash out and treat my family to a feast. I had purchased champagne from a boat which had sailed close by our cave, looking to offload its wares. I also purchased oranges from Seville and a goose from my good friend Samuel the poacher. We also had butter, cheese and milk from Mr Avery the farmer. Everyone received a present, and my little brothers and sisters squealed with delight at their gifts. They were mainly toys, considering most of them were children. But I had acquired a small dagger for my brother Charles, who was ecstatic with the gift, which pleased me a lot. To little Harry, I gave a toy boat. He played with that boat endlessly, and I believe he still has it to this day.

It was only my father who didn't celebrate the birth of our Lord with us. He sat by the fire, moaning about how it was not right for a lad so young to have such wealth. It must have been hard for him to see how easy life could be when you had the courage to speculate a little. He's mood didn't spoil the day for the rest of us though. My mother took me to one side, as the rest of the family ate, and sang merrily. Father would probably have liked solitude, but no one was letting him, and so eventually he cheered up and sang with the rest of us.

'Thank you for this John,' my mother said, embracing me with tears in her eyes.

'I wanted us to live like royalty for a change Ma. I've enjoyed it.' She held me at arm's length; almost studying me, so fierce was her gaze.

'My family are mostly gone now John. But when they lived, they shone brighter than the stars. I think you will outshine them all.' She looked over to father, as he hit a high note in a song with ease.

'Don't mind your father; he'd be miserable no matter what you did.' I wrapped my arms around her, and she protested when I picked her up and spun her around merrily. The drink I think had taken its toll.

When I put her down, she playfully hit me with a towel she always seemed to carry, and then looked at me seriously again. The extra candles I had purchased lit her face up into an almost angelic glow. She grasped my hand and squeezed it affectionately. 'I am glad you've found your calling my son; but just promise me one thing. Be careful; and don't get caught.'

In my mind I had felt untouchable and could not ever see myself falling into any bother which I couldn't get myself out of. Mother on the other hand had a look on her face that I had never seen before.

'I will be careful. I won't take any stupid chances, or risk's. Life is too good for that,' I said, laughing off the seriousness of the moment.

What I didn't know then when I made that promise, was that bother would find me soon enough. But in those early days, I felt as if I was riding the wave of success unhindered. Perhaps I was; but like any wave, it could all come crashing down if I was unlucky enough to sail the wrong one.

***

Christmas went by in a flash, just like all good times normally do. I was a young man with confidence in my intentions and money in my purse. My gifts to the family were lavish to say the least, considering our previous Christmases. I still had money enough to purchase a new shirt, trousers, overcoat and hat. The cost had been reasonable, coming to a total of just under three pounds. There was not much luxury to the garments, but they were of a finer quality than I had ever worn before. I helped the price by sweetening the deal with a few bottles of brandy. I always did that. For what it cost me, the gesture saved a fortune when I added a gift before payment.

Throughout the next year I turned my thoughts to learning all there was to know about smuggling. James and I would make notes and maps about the different coastlines we could sail to. We explored caves and made contacts with other smugglers, who thought it was amusing that lads like us were beginning to operate like seasoned professionals. I was introduced to rouges and gentlemen alike by John Vingoe, and we started to get our faces known in Penzance.

Smuggling was quite a common practice in those days, and many established crews were already well connected and left alone by the authorities.

I loved Penzance. It wasn't as busy as Falmouth, but the excitement and opportunity there kept boats and businesses thriving. It was at Penzance alas, where I had my first encounter with the customs men. It would turn out that they would plague me throughout my whole life.

My first encounter had to come sooner or later.

It had been a typical windy day. The clear blue sky and crisp morning air was welcome after a storm rocked the harbour the previous week. James and I had been lucky that we'd come into port when we did, or we could have found ourselves in real bother in our small boat.

Now the sea was calmer, we sailed out to do a bit of fishing. We had purchased nets early on to supplement our earnings, as well as legitimise our purpose at sea if ever we were questioned by the duty men. I liked fishing, and we would usually do quite well selling what we had before we even landed it ashore.

Buyers would come to fishermen, just as they pulled into the harbour, to secure the best fish and price before anybody else. The harbour as a result, had become an unofficial fish market. That day we sailed at great speed, and I shut my eyes relishing the wind and freedom. I had bought a pasty, which was a popular meal the miners liked to take with them. There is a large rolled crust of pastry to hold on to and discard once eaten. With hands as dirty as theirs would get, it was understandable why they threw it away. The one I had stuffed into my mouth was still warm from the baker's oven. A treat rarely experienced by a miner, who would have to eat it cold after hours wrapped in cloth. I still had their habit of throwing away the crust though, which the seagulls greedily gathered out of the water.

We watched the gulls often when we sailed. If they were very active in an area, it meant there would possibly be small fish below them. Small fish would obviously attract the bigger fish, which would try and gobble them up. They were the ones we were after and would fetch the biggest price.

I still had my eyes closed, feeling the gentle rocking of the waves. My senses were assaulted pleasantly by the nostalgic sea,

The King of Prussia Cove

when James shouted. 'What's that in the water; there John? Look over there, starboard.' I opened my eyes and looked starboard to see something bobbing in the water about a hundred yards away. James steered us closer, and we saw one of the gulls that had been following us land on the floating object.

'It's a barrel. Get the hook John! Pull it in.'

I quickly fetched a hook which we used for pulling in the bigger fish, while James manoeuvred the sloop around the floating barrel. Others on shore had caught sight of it as well, and I could see a few nearby boats coming our way to see what we had. We had to get to it fast, or it would most certainly be claimed by another opportunist like us.

We brought our sloop next to the barrel, and I rejoiced when I felt its weight at the end of my hook. James and I heaved to bring it on board, and it took both our efforts to do so. It was so heavy in fact that I nearly fell into the choppy water for our efforts.

After much straining, we managed to haul it on board and whooped to the sky when we discovered it was in fact brandy. I spotted a few more parcels of goods floating near the boat, and pulled them in.

There were about three in total, and all wrapped up in oilskins, keeping its contents water tight. I opened one and smelled the rich flavour of tobacco. It would have earned us a very pretty penny indeed. We put the tobacco parcels under a false floor I had made on the sloop and thanked providence for delivering us such luck.

We had been so occupied looking out towards the sea for more contraband, to see the danger darting towards us. We didn't know there was a small cutter swooping in behind us, until it shot a warning from one of its swivel guns, making me near jump out of my skin. I hadn't expected the noise, and its volume brought terror to us both. There were around six men rowing towards us, with muskets and pistols drawn.

'What do we do; shall we fight em?' James said tensely. They were no more than a few strokes away from our sloop. 'No. Not that; calm down and leave the talking to me,' I said to him calmer than I felt. Approaching were the dreaded customs men, and we were in trouble potentially. We had only found floating goods from a wrecked ship that would've washed up to shore eventually anyway.

'Let's just see what they have to say first eh,' I said more for myself. We were outmatched even if we did want to put up a fight.

'Prepare to be boarded by the king's men,' one shouted, as his men came on board our small sloop, and examined the barrel of brandy without asking us a thing. 'It's brandy sir!' he confirmed to a man who looked as high and mighty as the stupid wig he wore. The wind was making the flamboyant powdered piece flip up and down, and the man was forced to put a hand on it to stop it from blowing overboard. We knew who he was of course. Everyone in our profession knew him. He was hated by all smugglers and had made our capture and punishment of men of our ilk a crusade. His name was George Scrobel, a ruthless enforcer of his majesties revenue. There were many revenue men, but most were poor and uninterested with fighting with smugglers. Normally they were the dregs of the navy, who were poor seamen. Or those who were forced into the king's service by way of punishment.

George Scrobel was the exception to the badly organised and incompetent customs men. He revelled in the glory of a captured smuggler, and sold the booty for the king's benefit, aiding his own advancement. Most duty men didn't like a scrap with us, and I did not blame them for that really. Considering how much they were paid; the last thing they wanted to do was risk their lives catching us. George Scrobel on the other hand never shied away from a fight, and when I saw it was him on our boat my heart sank in despair.

I had to use every ounce of my wit to escape from the sorry encounter.

'Detain them in irons!' he ordered his men, who came upon us with clubs, and struck us with them savagely, even though we had not put up any resistance.

I was hit across the cheek hard and could feel it swelling painfully. We both curled into balls, and they beat us silly while we tried to fend them off, attempting to stop any serious blows

The King of Prussia Cove

caving our heads in. I then felt the irons go around my wrists, as we with the sloop, were taken back to port to face the unknown.

'I can explain myself if you would allow me sir,' I said through split lips, dripping blood and spittle onto the deck.

'I will warrant you could lad. But we have you banged to rights, make no mistake about that.'

He had a soft intelligent face, and cruel eyes. His men were reputed to dislike him for his willingness to put them in constant harm's way. The men with him today were all smiling though; and so, they should. It was a good day for them to catch a pair like us.

'We were just out fishing when we found the barrel floating towards us. We salvaged it on Lord Arundell's behalf,' I said to an uninterested Scrobel, who just sneered at me. I had heard of fishermen using this tactic before and hoped I would also get away with it.

I had noticed a gentleman in town who we knew to be one of Lord Arundel's agents. He was a big wig like most of the gentry, who emulated London's latest fashions. But now our fate would rest in his hands.

John Tonkin was known to be fair with the smuggling man and was active in the business himself as far as we had been told. He was an up and coming man from a very influential family in their own right.

John Tonkin in particular was being groomed by the Arundell's to become Mayor and Magistrate on their behalf. They wanted him to combat the Onslow-Borlace threat to the office.

I hoped, as we came back to town, that he could help us in our dire predicament.

'I was to give the barrel to Mr Tonkin sir. If you would just ask him, I'm sure he can straighten this matter out,' I repeated my plea of innocence desperately. The mention of the name Tonkin caught his interest, and he walked over to me, bringing his face inches from my own. I could smell his rancid breath, which was worse than fish guts. 'We shall see him; but it won't do you two any good. You will hang for this you know,' he answered me cruelly.

We were led to the customs house, and a man was sent to fetch Mr Tonkin to ascertain the truth of our claim. We waited for about half an hour; long enough to make us sweat. John Tonkin arrived at last and walked in as though he owned the place. He was of medium height and was popular with the ladies because of his charm and handsome appearance. He had a slightly powdered face and wore a black beauty spot to hide a scar he had suffered from the pox as a child. His expression was neutral, and I could not guess which way he would go. 'Why are these men detained?' He asked firmly.

'They said they claimed an anker of brandy for the Lord Arundel, and mentioned it was for you sir. But I think they're just smuggling vermin, robbing from the king's pockets.'

Mr Tonkin smiled the most charming of smiles, but not in humour. It was the kind of predatory smile that seemed to unnerve George Scrobel. 'They speak the truth, and you were right to bring them to me,' He announced in an even and cultured voice. 'Why are they bruised and bloodied, did they resist arrest?'

Scrobel would not apologise for doing what he thought was his duty.

'I believe they have smuggled that brandy sir, and they will face the consequences for their actions. How did you even know that barrel was out their sir?' Scrobel inquired. He squinted his pale blue eyes, which were colder and unforgiving as the merciless sea, waiting for the gentlemen to slip up. 'These two told me they had spotted something this morning, and I bid them to salvage it for the Arundell family, who as you well know hold salvage and wrecking rights here.' Scrobel shook his head not buying Tonkin's story one bit. He knew he would not win the battle against Lord Arundell if his agent had claimed the goods on his behalf. But it clearly irked him to let us slip through his net.

'If they are your men Mr Tonkin, then what are their names?' I had thought Scrobel had finally out thought us. But God had once again put me in this situation for a reason, because he answered without a pause. 'John Carter of course; his friend I don't know, but they work together, and help me sometimes in matters such as

The King of Prussia Cove

this. So be a good man and take off those irons.' I didn't have a clue how he knew my name. I couldn't very well ask him in front of the revenue men, who had very little choice but to let us go on our merry way.

I felt the urge to run out of the building. Its low ceilings and dingy atmosphere gave me a turn. I resisted the feeling and as James and I left, I heard Mr Tonkin say to us. 'Now don't forget you two; take that anker of brandy to my ship The Glory. Then I'll meet you both at the Turks Head Inn as we agreed.' We nodded and went on our way as fast as we could.

Scrobel looked furious when we left. Our paths would cross many times after that day, but the Lord had blessed me once again, and set my course in a new and prosperous direction. He had sent me my guardian angel Mr John Tonkin.

CHAPTER 6

After we loaded the salvaged spirits on board the large ninety-ton cutter named The Glory. We made our way to the Turks Head Inn, battered and bruised from our ordeal. As we entered, I immediately noticed John Tonkin seated with another fellow named Mr Treluddra, who also worked on behalf of the Arundell family. He caught sight of us through the smoky haze and beckoned us over to his table. We sat down, and must have looked like urchins because the state we were in.

'You two were nearly for the rope you know,' he told us cheerfully. 'I am in your debt sir. Thank you.' His partner smoked a pipe, and was blowing rings, which slid around the peak of his hat to mingle with the cloud of smog above. 'Those bloody revenue men are a curse on us lad. Well done for spotting that anker and claiming it for the Lord Arundell. He will be pleased, I'm sure.' Mr Treluddra was not part of the gentry. He was too rough around the edges for that. His attire suited his character perfectly. He was smartly turned out in a light brown coat and

The King of Prussia Cove

trousers. He held a silver topped cane which rested by his side to demonstrate that he was wealthier than he looked.

'Is the brandy on my ship lad?' Mr Tonkin said to me in particular. 'It is sir. But if I may ask, how you knew my name when the customs man questioned you?' He beamed a smile at me, showing off perfect white teeth such as I had. 'I make it my business to know young man. I have heard very good things about you. For someone as young as you are, I'm amazed you are doing so well. But I was an early starter as well. I wish you good luck Master Carter.' I took that as an ending of our meeting.

However, I could see an opportunity in that moment and decided to chance my arm a little further. 'I beg your pardon sir, but could I ask another favour of you?' His eyebrows rose, almost to suggest I was pushing my luck. He humoured me though.

'I thought saving your life today was boon enough lad.' Mr Treluddra prompted me to speak. 'So, what else do you want Master Carter?'

I wanted the whole world, and if my request was granted it would place me in the right direction to have it.

'I want to present the barrel of brandy to Lord Arundell personally, if he will allow it. We rent a farm on his land you see, and I have always wished to meet with him.' They both burst out laughing at the cheek of my request. There I was, a young lad who had just ducked out of the clutches of the duty officers, now asking to meet the Lord of the land. 'I think he would be amused by that, don't you Mr Treluddra.'

'I do Mr Tonkin, I do.'

***

We made our way to the large estate, where Lord Arundell dwelled in utter luxury and pomp at a place called Trerice, near Newquay. He did laugh, just as they said he would. Mr Tonkin told him all about our adventure in comical detail. The Lady Arundell also heard the story and rushed out into the entrance hall of their enormous house to meet us. While I waited, I could not help but be awed and impressed with the furniture and finery around us. The high ceilings had golden painted stars among a rich blue background. There was mahogany furniture everywhere, and detailed rugs that had come from the Far East. I could see intricate china vases and statues of old leaders from ancient times. There were also portraits of the many Arundell family members, dating back to before the 13th century.

One painting caught my eye in particular. It was of Fredrick of Prussia. I did not know why he had that ruler's portrait in his house, but it was not surprising. The great King of Prussia was famous for his military tactics and personality. He had become most popular and fascinated me.

I was admiring the artwork when Lord and Lady Arundell descended their great staircase, which led down to the entrance hallway where we waited. I was very aware about my beaten-up appearance, but they didn't grimace at my sorry state when Mr Tonkin introduced me formally to them. 'Oh… I thought there were two of them.' Lady Arundell said serenely. She had a small fan which she fluttered at her powdered face, and she waved it around as she spoke.

'The other lad is waiting outside my Lady. It was only Master Carter who wished to meet with your graces.' James was waiting with Mr Treluddra outside in the grounds of the Arundell's estate. He'd told me he felt uncomfortable going before the presence of the gentry.

'I wouldn't know what to say John. Anyway, it was your dumb idea to meet with them. What were you thinking?' he had moaned to me on our way here. I had thought about the opportunity it could be, to operate with the blessing of one of the most powerful families in Cornwall. I was also thinking that my charm could cross over the class lines, and that people were people no matter what their station.

I bowed graciously to them both, and they nodded with smiles on their faces at the entertainment I was providing. The wigs they wore were like status symbols of power. Wigs after all were

The King of Prussia Cove

expensive items. Her wig was white like a winter's frost, and so high it sat, that she seemed even taller than me.

'Do you like the painting?' Lord Arundell asked. 'I noticed you admiring it.' His wig was flat, as was the current fashion for the gentry at the time, but no less intricate. His false ponytail was tied with a blue ribbon of fine quality, and no doubt cost a fortune.

'I am a great admirer of King Fredrick my Lord. They have a portrait of him in the Ship Inn at Porthleven. It's not as fine a picture as this one, I must declare, but I like the stories I hear about him.' He moved away from his wife to stand beside me and looked at the portrait with a scholarly expression. 'He is a great man that is true.' We discussed the Prussian monarch briefly, and it was clear by how animated he was in talking on the subject, that I knew I was off to a good start. He eventually changed the subject smoothly.

'I understand you have some salvaged brandy for me.' I nodded at him happily and went over the story of what had happened to us. I didn't mention the fact, that if we had not been caught, the brandy would've been sold within the day with the coin going straight into our pockets.

'I thank you for your service. I wish I had more honest men like yourself you know.' At that point I produced my surprise which I'd concealed secretly into a sown pocket inside my jacket.

John Tonkin's eyes went wide and looked like he was about to step in front of me. He told me afterwards that he thought I was pulling out a weapon of some sorts to attack the Lord and Lady with.

When I pulled out the several oil skinned parcels, they all looked at me curiously. 'What is that?' Lady Arundell said as I opened the parcel theatrically. 'I also retrieved this from the water, and it's completely dry and still fine to smoke my Lord. I wanted to gift this to you personally, as a thank you for your Lordship for keeping the rent so fair on our farm. Of course, I am also grateful for the service that Mr Tonkin has done for me; and so, I also present one to you.' I said and pulled out another parcel for John Tonkin.

The fact of the matter was, Lord Arundell had claim to all the salvage, as was his right. But he did not protest when I handed over the tobacco to his agent. I would even say they looked pleased with my surprised gift. 'Splendid young man... just splendid. Many a man would have kept that to themselves. I thank you again and commend you for your conduct today,' he said cheerfully.

'Is fishing your only occupation Carter?' he asked with one eyebrow raised; knowing already that I was a smuggler. His agent and my saviour would most certainly have told him. So instead of lying, I came right out with it.

'Well I've been known to acquire certain goods from time to time sir, if you catch my meaning.'

No one seemed surprised by my admission, and there was an obvious shared interest in the activity. He told me that he hated the customs men, who would always fight against his right to wreckages.

I told him of my ambition, and how I was currently enterprising and growing my trade every day. Both he and even the Lady Arundell appeared tremendously impressed with my personal account, that when I had finished portraying my own dream, he replied to me as if he had just thought it.

'How would you like to help me out from time to time?' It was hard not to smile at his acceptance of me. 'I would be delighted my Lord.'

'Excellent idea my Lord; we could use someone with courage and wits like Mr Carter here. I foresee you will go far, and I am rarely wrong you know,' prophesied Tonkin to me; clearly pleased with the way I had conducted myself.

'Yes. I must show my appreciation young man; for the goods you have salvaged for us.'

I could have earned a great sum of money for what I had brought him that day. The brandy alone would have sold at four pounds or so. But I wanted to make allies, so declined his offer humbly. 'I'm just happy that I've done you a service my Lord and hope I can again.' The gesture I made was clear, and he shook my hand with a firm grip. He never shook the hand of the common man I learned

The King of Prussia Cove

latter. I must have made an impression. 'Very well young Carter, I'll tell you what. Let me decrease the rent of the farm this year to say a pound.' We paid him two pounds a year for our small place. It would relieve the burden tremendously on my father, who had recently become ill, and suffered with his breathing badly. He had been so stubborn that he kept returning to work day after day, despite his failing health.

'My father will be most grateful my Lord,' I said, excepting his generosity. We left the house and I couldn't believe what had happened to me. Mr Tonkin climbed on his horse and James and I walked the short journey back to Penzance via a well-worn path. 'You have impressed me,' Mr Tonkin said from his horse. 'I have a larger sloop that will crew about ten men being built. I will sell it to you, on very reasonable credit terms. But tell me, do you know the Guernsey ports well?' I did and told him of our daring trips in our small sloop, which I shared with James, who had not said much on our way back. 'Wonderful; I need some cargo collected in a few months' time, and it would be useful to have honest lads collecting for me. Do you think you can handle a boat that size John?' he said as an afterthought. James answered for me, finding his voice at last.

'I can sir. I've been a seaman for years now.' Mr Tonkin clapped his hands together at our arrangement, and we discussed the rest of the details on the way back to Penzance.

I have sailed to many countries in my time, but as we journeyed along the coastal path, I marvelled at the rugged beauty of my home county. There was nowhere in the world I could imagine living at the time. John Tonkin shared my love of Cornwall.

I will never forget being on the road with that man who saved us from the noose. Though we were classes apart, and he was sixteen years my senior, I got on well and liked him from the offset. It was plain he liked me too. He would often boast about my antics in the beer houses and about town, which did my reputation a world of good both as a smuggler, and honest dealer.

***

It was so important in our occupation to be seen as honest. If I agreed to do something for someone; I did it.

If they ordered goods from me, then I would deliver on time and with a smile on my face. They came back to me every time consequently. There were numerous other smugglers a person could buy their duty-free goods from. But most were ill tempered, and not very agreeable. People would here about me and tell their friends that I dealt a straight hand.

James spoke up to me when we had parted company from our new friends and told me his concerns. He was shaken up from our near-death experience. 'I don't know John,' he said sullenly. 'We might be biting more than we can chew if we start collecting on this scale.' He was happy with our small-time operation and wanted to keep it that way.

If I hadn't met him, James would've happily distributed contraband to the good folk of Helston until his dying day. That wasn't for me though. I was too ambitious, and impatient. But the truth was I couldn't expand and grow without him. 'I'll tell you what James; if I left you to take care of our interests with the Vingoe's, making the odd run over to Guernsey. We can double our efforts and our profits. Anything I make collecting Mr Tonkin's goods, I'll split with you half way, and you do the same for me.' He liked the idea but complained that he would struggle to distribute all the goods by himself, and he was correct in saying so. I couldn't operate alone either. 'We need to recruit more lads,' I said.

'Bringing in more people would hurt our profits man,' he said, always the pessimist. He couldn't see that more men would only add more distribution, and more wealth.

'We can pay them a percentage of the profits; say five percent for their wage and cut. Then we take the rest. More lads out there will mean more deals with more people, and more coins in our purse.' Eventually I broke him, and he bought into the idea when I made him see just how profitable we would be by running the two operations. So, he took our small sloop back to Porthleven, and

The King of Prussia Cove

began to recruit some of his friends to help, both on the boat, and as our main distributors around the area. I did the same, and I knew exactly where to go to find sailors to crew my new sloop. It just so happened that the ones in mind were at the harbour that very day. Another blessing I had mused.

My Uncle on my mother's side was a fisherman who had worked out of Penzance for years. He had a small cottage along Mounts Bay, where he and my cousins were making a reasonable living from fishing, wrecking and a bit of smuggling. His name was Henry and I met him in the Admiral Benbow, which was a popular beer house in town. I asked him if he could spare any sailing men for good pay. Fortunately, he and his son had argued with each other constantly, and he was grateful to be shot of him.

'It may only be for one voyage though. You may have to take him back,' I said light heartedly. 'A break from his company, even a temporary one, would be a blessing John,' he admitted.

If I hadn't helped the Vingoe's I would have ended up asking that very man, my uncle for a job on his crew.

I never thought that nearly a year later, I would be asking him if he had any lads to work for me.

'Your mother must be proud of you; to do such things at your age.' I heard people say that so often. I didn't mind; I liked to surprise them. If somebody like my father told me that I couldn't do something; it spurned me on more to attain it. 'She is proud Uncle. I don't go home as much as I would like. This life certainly keeps you busy,' I said, and clinked cups with him to toast our agreement. I would take his boy on, who was about three years older than me. He was an experienced sailor with tremendous skill at the steering oar and could navigate the coast of France and Guernsey expertly. He also gave me the names of some dimwits who knew their way around a sloop. They were strong to load and unload cargo, but good for nothing else.

I had my crew, my navigator and my patron, John Tonkin, who brought me to the sloop he was helping me purchase. 'Mr Carter, she's your sloop. You can pay me back in instalments on credit. Don't bloody sink her hey lad. She will still need paying for you know.' I looked her over, and I was overjoyed that this was at my disposal. It had a smooth hull, and was not overlapped like most boats, so it would cut through the water like a hot knife through butter. It was also fore and aft rigged, which enabled it to sail across or against the wind if need be. This made it highly manoeuvrable and for a smuggler it could very well save your life. For if you came into a cove at high tide and the wind was in the wrong direction, you would be stranded on the sand and easy pickings for pirates and the dreaded duty men. They were often frustrated by the superior ships of the smuggling man. They would usually have square rigged sails, which could only travel with the wind on their backs, and mostly sailed in diagonal lines. Their overlapping planks would also slow them down to a degree, where we would run rings around their heavy oak sloops.

The one I would sail in was made from fir, her triangle sails would aid us with speed, and would be useful for in shore work. She was a fine thirty-two-ton sloop.

'What will you call her?' he asked me. I had never named anything before, but I knew exactly what she would be called.

'The Endeavour,' I whispered reverently; as if I were naming my first child.

'An apt name, for a fine vessel,' he declared just as solemnly. John Tonkin like me, was young, ambitious and was looking to make his name.

We toasted our deal, and then went over all the boring but necessary details.

With my crew assembled, and my cargo waiting at the docks of Guernsey, I set out to begin my voyage to collect.

The contraband was all paid for at the other end, so we didn't need to carry over money, which could have been lost, stolen or sent to the bottom of the sea. I learned on that first trip, in my new boat that my uncle had not been exaggerating about my cousin, who was also named Henry. He whined and moaned all day and night, but strangely seemed all the happier for it. He must have been. No one could be that miserable I thought. His ability at sea on the other hand was an acceptable compromise for the annoyance. He was an absolute wonder and a master sailor. He was worth his weight in gold in the end. He was also fluent in the French language, which he was kind enough to teach me.

I was a keen pupil too, and would suck in information like a sponge, it didn't take me long at all to become a competent speaker of French and was near fluent within the year, thanks to that miserable cousin.

Henry liked me though. Especially when I gave him his large percentage from the profits we made on our numerous trips to Guernsey.

The port on that day was busy, and the activity normally started early, as men would get drunk through to the evening. It was a small miracle that, so much brandy and gin made it over to our country when I witnessed the drinking in Guernsey.

Our cargo was mercifully waiting for us at the dock side, and Mr Tonkin's agent, Harry Price, directed the cargo to come on board. Loading was easy but worked up a keen thirst, and Most of the lads were reluctant to head back immediately. I also wanted to have a chat with Mr Price. So, I headed off to a nearby inn where we could bed down for the night and have a good drink to calm the nerves.

Old George Scrobel was on my mind a great deal that night, and I touched the small scare he had so kindly gifted me on my face, which made me look older than I was. In addition, my appearance did have the benefit to make me seem tough and rugged.

I looked like a proper brawler with my battle wounds.

This helped to gain the respect of my small crew, who had seen me fight in town on occasion and none had argued against my wishes. They moaned plenty. But any crew on board with old misery guts Henry was bound to follow suit, and so they did.

The effect was likewise when we sat to drink at an inn that night. Men gave me a wide berth and ladies perched on my knee. I questioned Mr Price at length on how the whole operation worked.

There were many ways a man could earn a sum from smuggling. What we did for the Vingoe's for example had been purely distribution, but profitable none the less.

'The real money is in the larger cargos,' Mr Price explained to me. 'What you are doing for the Tonkin family will earn them a fortune from this one batch alone. Lots of men from England and all around the coast, from Essex to Yorkshire, are at it in some shape or form. The Dutch ports are even busier than this one.'

It was true that, so many small-time crews like me were buying contraband from the continent and selling it for ridicules prices back home. Here you could buy an Anker of gin for one pound and sell it for four pounds to the English innkeepers and beer houses; and that was before it was watered down.

Tea, tobacco and pepper were even more lucrative, and smugglers had to think of imaginative ways to get it past the ever-vigilant duty men.

Sometimes, tobacco was made into ropes, and then casually thrown on the deck, or hung innocently in plain sight. They put false floors in barrels of water or wine, which carried a much smaller duty; but the customs men became wise to this and started measuring depths with dipping rods.

The famous smuggling Coopers came up with many ingenious ways to get the contraband past inspection.

To beat the dipping rods, they would make diagonal compartments inside the barrels and packed them full of goods, right under the authority's noses.

I wasn't ready at the time to purchase on the same scale as Mr Tonkin. I would have to collect and distribute for financers like him, until I could afford it on my own.

My mind greedily calculated my cut from the voyage. I hoped that it would be the first of many such journeys, but we still had to get it back home after all.

CHAPTER 7

The landing off the goods and distribution was my specialty.

I was becoming a half decent sailor, with encyclopaedic knowledge of both the English and French coastlines. But dealing with people was what I loved the most. I had suggested to Mr Tonkin that we land the goods from Guernsey, at a cove I frequented with James at Porthleah.

It was equidistant from Penzance and Helston, so distribution would be easier in both directions. A brewess there went by the name of Bessie and ran a beer house which was on top of the cliffs.

It was remote, isolated from all but a few local men, and perfect for smuggling operations. That was where we would land our cargo, and I had told John Tonkin about the location. He just so happened to know the owner of the land at Porthleah, which was conveniently Lord Arundell. I would make a point to ask his permission to rent it from him upon our return from Guernsey.

When crossing the channel, heading for home; we spotted a few customs boats on the horizon, but they didn't worry us in the slightest. We easily out ran them with our superior sloop and crew.

Once they realised that they couldn't keep up, they backed off for easier pickings.

We would still have to be sure not to be careless when we unloaded our cargo. That would be the most dangerous time for any smuggler, normally with nowhere to run. As we approached our destination, we all stopped any kind of joking and mirth and cruised into the cove, just as the sun began to set.

The cove itself was split into three, and the one we were headed for was named after the brewess herself, Bessie's cove. I could see the beer house windows glow with candlelight, as the darkness drew in, aiding our stealth like approach. I knew Bessie would be pleased to see me, especially if I had some spirit and ale to sell.

An agent of John Tonkin met me at the natural slipway. Its smooth rocky surface led into the cove making it the perfect launch and landing spot for us.

We sweated profusely, even though the early evening had a slight chill in the air. It was hard work getting the many barrels and parcels into the caves dotted around the cove. But I think we all sweated mainly for fear of capture. I had never landed that much cargo before, and I constantly looked to the hills above for customs riders, and out to the sea where the sun was tranquilly setting over the western horizon, casting us all in an ethereal glow. I am a lover of such beauty normally. I could watch a sunset or sunrise forever, and never tire of it. This one I barely noticed though, as I watched tensely for our doom to arrive.

My panic was not necessary in the end. Eventually we landed it all without any damage or drama, and took our payment from the agent, to which I then spread out among the lads. My cut and Henry's were the largest of course, and I must say, I had never done so well in all my life until that point. My crew were pleased also, and we stayed at Bessie's place that night. She very kindly relieved us of some of our new wealth. But oh, what a night that was. I was lorded over by the lads for the success of the voyage, and Bessie and her daughter Marie came over to congratulate me for bringing in such an amount of cargo. They had purchased a few barrels straight from the boat, and we sat at a table and chatted for hours.

'It's perfect here,' I said to Bessie, who poured another gin into my cup. 'It's so isolated; you wouldn't see a two-hundred-ton cutter unless you looked right over the cliffs edge. It's perfect,' I repeated, and rubbed my hands together. 'You're welcome to come back here as much as you like John. I know Marie would like that,' Bessie said mischievously trying to embarrass her daughter, who was a curvaceous beauty with a wit as strong as her mother.

Marie just smiled coyly and rubbed my leg with her feet under the table. The night was getting better and better. 'Yes. I would like that indeed,' Marie confirmed, and moved in, giving me a drunken kiss. For my sins I enjoyed it.

'I would like to set up a permanent base here if you wouldn't mind Bess,' I asked her, seeking blessing out of respect. I knew she wouldn't mind, considering the amount of cheap goods that would flow through her establishment. It would bring risk to her little corner of paradise. But Bessie loved the idea. Being a widow of a smuggler herself, she happily agreed to my proposal of using the cove as my staging post for future operations. 'As long as you lads keep coming to spend some coin, I'll be a happy woman,' she confirmed, just before I passed out.

***

The next day I had the worst effects from drinking I've ever had. My long hair had come loose and was matted in vomit. I walked to the sea to wash the worst off, and the effort of it nearly drowned me.

My crew were in no better shape than I, and I watched them all come down to the cove to empty their stomachs. We were all heavy drinkers in those days, until I leaned away from my sinful ways, and turned to the light of God.

After I recovered it was time to get back to work.

It was my first big shipment, with a new crew, who looked at my youth initially as a weakness. After that voyage, they came to

The King of Prussia Cove

respect my ability to lead them. They had been sold on my dream of becoming rich and wealthy, and like any good skipper, I distributed the coin promised, promptly and fairly. I have always operated in this fashion and my reputation for honest dealings secured the loyalty of sellers, customer and crew.

During the following months I made my enquiries to rent the land at Porthleah.

Now known to Lord Arundell, the matter was straight forward, and his agent Mr Treluddra gave me permission to use the area for residential or fishing activities. They all knew the reality of the use of the land of course. In fact, I made it my business to pay a contribution from all my smuggling profits to Lord Arundell. He was not expecting the extra payments, and the gesture worked wonders for my status, as well as his patronage.

It was Mr Tonkin's idea to wet the beak of the Arundell family. 'Basically lad; he was impressed when he met you, and he doesn't get impressed easily. Do yourself a favour and cross his palm with some of your profit from time to time. It will go a long way, believe me,' he said.

'Do you pay him?' I asked, passively.

'I do lad; I pay him handsomely in fact. I pay him, and he helps me, and my family acquire status. It's the way business works you know. One hand washing the other and so forth,' he said as a matter of fact.

So, I paid the Arundell's handsomely out of my share of the profits. I had the largest cut after all, and I was the one who wanted his favour.

I also wanted to make a name for myself, just like John Tonkin had. He was at the time being groomed to become mayor of Penzance by the Arundell's, which would benefit me by association. It would become a profitable relationship, all built upon the foundations of those early deals and payments.

When I was given permission to stay at Porthleah, I purchased a small amount of timber and constructed a tiny structure to rest in. It was nothing grand; only as big as two men lying down really. But it was shelter enough for the time being.

I remember a messenger from home coming one day when we were constructing the roof.

It had been a fair while since I had been back at the farm, so I jumped down eager for any news from Charles who was the bearer of it.

He ran to me with cheeks puffed red from the exertion of his journey. 'Why such haste brother?' I said concerned. He stopped before me and took a knee. Breathlessly, he tried to speak his message, only to flounder with the words. 'Breathe Charles; that's it. Now what's the matter?'

'It's father... he's dying John,' he answered me at last, still gasping for air. He had tried to run the whole way to the cove, which was many miles to say the least. 'Come on brother; you must be exaggerating. What do you mean he's dying?' I stood there unconvinced.

'His lungs are worse John; much worse. The Ferret and the Godolphin's have forced him down the mine when he was barely able to stand. It's near finished him off. He has asked for you.'

I knew my father had a bad cough which was becoming worse and worse each year. But dying? I couldn't believe Charles, so I hurried as fast as I could back home.

The house when I arrived, was humid and had a smell of sickness I recognised immediately. I looked over to a bed where my father lay as white as ash. He wheezed with every breath he took. Most of the family saw the good sense to stay outside of the house. Only my mother and my two sisters remained, and were fussing around, trying to be helpful in some way.

I placed my hand on his pale, cold brow.

'Father!' I said, trying to get his attention. His eyes were wild with delirium, and I took his hand and gripped it tight.

'Father it's me John.' His eyes snapped to mine urgently.

'John... Thank God you came; I can feel the Lord taking me.' He coughed up a mouthful of phlegm and spat it into a spittoon next to his bed. 'Come on Father, you're not dying. You're just sick, that's all. Where's all of that Carter stubbornness.'

I wished my words were true. But seeing him, I knew he was dying. I couldn't tell him that, even if he knew it himself. My mother came over and placed a warm, damp cloth on his brow. 'Thank you, Agnes,' he said to her weakly. 'I'm glad I got the chance to see you before the end son.' He coughed some more as he spoke. It was hard for him to breathe, let alone speak to me. But he would say his piece, despite my protestations for him to rest quietly.

'There's no time for that now lad. I've told your brothers and sisters what I expect of them when I'm gone, and now it's your turn.' I could hear my mother weeping in the background, and I turned to see one of my sisters comforting her. Father squeezed my hand lightly and gave me his final advice. I had never listened to him before and expected much of the same from him.

'I was wrong about you son... I wanted you to go down the mine and support your own family one day from that honest work. I've been hearing things about what you've been getting up to of late. Truth be told, I didn't approve one bit. I realise now, the shafts were not what God had in store for you. There's too much adventure in you lad for that kind of work. Too much of your mother eh...' I had not expected to hear those words come from his mouth. 'I am proud of the young man you've become,' he added.

'Why did they let you go down there, if they knew you were sick?' I said to him angrily. I hated the Godolphin's in that moment. 'They only care about profits John. They worked me like a pack horse and they could not care less what happens to us when we brake. Your brothers and sisters have been dismissed too.' The farm I fear is in deep jeopardy lad.'

'Don't worry about that. I'll take care of the family now father; and the Godolphin's. That Ferret will get his comeuppance as well. I swear he will.' He shook his head violently. 'No... The Lord says to love thy enemy boy. Besides, a gentleman like that would ruin the likes of us, if the whim took him.' I would not agree with him but nodded anyway. He didn't need my anger in the condition he was in. But I would seek revenge for his treatment. I was making some powerful friends of my own, and I wouldn't stand their treatment of my kin.

I sat with father through the night; my mother too.

She was exhausted from caring for him and the farm. At dawn, he passed into Gods hands, leaving us to weep over his body in terrible grief. At least I got to see him before the end. At least I finally had his blessing, which was no consolation to me until years later.

With the family out of work, it was now my responsibility to look after them.

It just so happened I had work for everyone. I was expanding nicely and was going to ask Charles sooner or later if he would come to Porthleah to work at the cove and on my sloop.

I had an errand to run first though. Something was compelling me to act. I knew I was partly responsible for my family's treatment at the hands of the Godolphin's. The prank I pulled on him had been a stupid one, and as my father lay cold, waiting for burial at our local church yard. I headed off for my vengeance.

***

I journeyed to Porthleven the same day spoiling for a fight, hoping to bump into the Godolphin family. I especially wanted to find the Ferret. He had most certainly had a hand in my father and family's ill treatment.

I wandered around from beer house to beer house, even managing to do a bit of business with some folk who wanted to purchase contraband. As I was drinking myself stupid, he walked in bold and grinning rotten teeth.

'Eh… Ferret! I want a word with you,' I shouted from my table. The place had been quite merry before my outburst, and everyone stopped at the sudden drama. In the silence, Arthur Ferris walked to the bar with his eye twitching nervously. With his back facing me I stood and stomped over to him to speak my mind. Maybe if I had not been so drunk, I would have been more amicable, and things may not have gone so far. But I was in a fighting mood that night, and the focus of my anger had just walked right into my path.

'I said… I want to talk to you.' I grabbed his long coat and turned him violently. Everyone in the Inn made room expecting a fight.

'I have nothing to say to the likes of you. We are better off, to be shot of you and the rest of your family Carter. Now bugger off,' he said to me defiantly.

I would not be cast aside so easily though and stopped him from turning back towards the bar.

I have said before that I was big and powerful. I was naturally so. Many Carters were.

The years of toil down the mines had added layers of muscle to my already strong body, and with it, I held him where he stood with little effort. He was about ten years older than me but briefly, I saw fear in his squinting eyes.

'Get your hands off me boy!' he demanded, trying to be as menacing as possible. 'Just to let you know Ferret. My father died this morning. You made him go down there, even though he was sick. You fined him, and stopped his pay, and now you have dismissed my whole family. I just wanted to know how you can live with yourself.' He just laughed in my face as I held him at arm's length. 'He's dead then? One less Carter I suppose,' he said without compassion.

I hit him hard on the jaw without further word. He would have dropped down, but I held him up and hit him again, breaking his nose with another solid punch. I let him fall; holding his heavily bleeding nose.

'Bastard… A pox on you, ya bloody Bastard!' he shouted from the wooden floor. He reached hastily into his coat and pulled a knife, pointing it straight at me.

The room had turned deathly quiet now and everyone waited to see how the tussle would conclude. I was a good fighter, but I wasn't that keen on risking a knife in the belly.

In the silence I heard a pistol slowly being cocked. The Ferret must have heard it too, and he hesitated.

To my relief, Samuel the poacher had come to my rescue with a steady pistol aimed calmly at my opponent.

'I would drop that if I were you Arthur. I don't want any misfortune to befall you tonight.' He came and stood next to me with a face like steel. He was a crack shot with pistol, bow or musket, and the Ferret, like all local men knew it. They had all been buying meat from Samuel for years after all. Arthur's eyes darted from me to him rapidly, deciding whether to attack or not. He wasn't drunk like I was, and wisely placed the knife on the bar.

'You will both pay for this. Mark my words. You two are done around here,' he threatened bitterly and spat blood at our feet.

He left humiliated, with his head low in shame and defeat. I knew he would not stop until he got his own back. Unfortunately, it wouldn't be long before we met again.

Once he was gone the place erupted with an almighty cheer. No one liked him, and the story would be told for years to come.

'My word John, you sure did catch him. What a punch!' said Robert Hatton, the butcher. Most folk in town I had dealt with at one time or another, and all came over to compliment my actions. I had many a drink bought for me until James Thomas, my partner came by and took me and Samuel away and to bed.

CHAPTER 8

I woke up around midday when the innkeeper knocked on the door to see if we planned on staying another night. I declined, rubbing my head as James came into the room. 'You know that little stunt last night could harm our business John,' he said to me earnestly. I told him the whole story, and he understood then that I had no choice but to confront the man who had treated my family with such contempt.

'Is he ever going to wake up?' James indicated to Samuel, who was still snoring loudly from the floor where he slept. I laughed at how events had escalated the night before and tried to shake him awake. 'Leave me damn you,' he told me irritated.

'We could use a man like him John. Someone as skilled as he is with weapons would help us greatly if we get into a bit of bother with the duty men. It's only a matter of time after all.' That was true.

They were becoming more and more active. If we wanted to keep our liberty, then we would need to defend ourselves and our cargo with force.

The King of Prussia Cove

I made a note to ask Samuel if he would come and work for us. But before that, I had to bury my farther.

***

The funeral took place at our church and drew in a crowd larger than most folks had seen in a long time. He was an honest and decent man my father, and I shook the hands of many of his friends and relatives that day.

We sang hymns, and later went back to Porthleven to reminisce over past times with those who knew him best. No one from the Godolphin family came in sight, and it was just as well they did not. My mood was dark still, and I feared what I would do to any foe who crossed my path.

I stayed with some friends for a few days after that near Helston, when some good news finally came to break me out of my melancholy.

A ship had been wrecked in the stormy seas, not far from where I lodged, causing an exodus of excited people to clear it of its cargo. I virtually flew there, so I could arrive before any of the gentry could make a claim.

I could hardly blame the poor villager, who swarmed like bees over honey around the wreckage. The working men and women of Cornwall did not have much in their lives and jumped at the chance to get their hands on anything valuable.

Most people would struggle from year to year, lucky to have food and shelter. They prayed for a wreck and believed God had churned the sea and wind to bring them respite from their miserable lives.

It was hard to watch the unfortunate sailors swim to shore and cling on to rocks with desperation and fear etched on their faces. As opposed to the paradox of the locals, who launched small boats and rowed out to the now abandoned ship with utter glee. Some were even swimming out to pull in the many barrels which floated around temptingly.

There were many injured in the attempt, and sadly, a few men drowned. But the reward was too great for them to just wait for the wealthy men to come and take away their wreck. They would risk the ultimate price to claim a piece of it.

I must declare that I was among their ranks, and brought with me a pack horse, a few lads who worked for me and loaded the beast of burden to the utmost capacity.

James swung around in our sloop and made short runs to a nearby cave we used, and we kept on making runs until the wreck had been cleaned out bare. It took only twenty-four hours to relieve it of its cargo; a feat seemingly impossible to outsiders.

George Borlace even wrote a letter to parliament, describing how the Dutch wreck was cleared of claret within a day of succumbing to the rocks. He and his men tried to retake what they could from the poor folk, but that task was harder than prising food from a starving man's hand.

The authorities turned up that day, as they would do for any wreck. But they wouldn't dare to interfere, or make any arrests, for fear of their own lives. Locals after all did not take kindly to any interference, and they knew it.

The customs officer who'd arrested me before had tried to interfere once when he was young and ambitious. He managed to walk away from his poor decision with a cut to his face, and a ferocious beating.

Now even he would not get between a wreck and the wreckers. They were mainly tinners, and labourers from nearby. A few smuggling crews also turned up after we had cleared the majority away. But they didn't begrudge us our spoils.

It was a kind of first come, first claim scenario, which was respected by most. We would sell them some of what we salvaged anyway, so they would not lose out too badly.

'This will set us up John. We've got nigh on the whole cargo,' James said joyfully as we sailed to the caves where we had hidden the claret and other goods in our usual cunning fashion. No one would find it, and I went to work immediately to distribute what we had.

James was correct in saying it would set us up; that one wreck would help our efforts to expand wondrously. We employed lads from the local farms, and disgruntled urchins who jumped at the chance to earn some decent pay.

For a week in the field they could earn about seven shillings; and that was hard to live on I can tell you.

But for one night's work distributing and ferrying my cargo, I paid five shillings.

Oh, they all loved a man who paid well. For that pay was guaranteed. A man can make or break himself by his reputation. Mine began in those early days of my smuggling and fishing.

If I made a promise to deliver goods to someone, I would deliver it at the specified time agreed. I was very hands on, and would reward my lads, so my standards were upheld to the letter.

The same reliability was extended to paying men or women who worked for me. They would always be paid on time, and they loved me for it.

The farm owners always complained when I fleeced them of some of their best workers. But I would just give them a good deal on ale or sweeten them up with a parcel of goods every now and then to grease the wheels of progress.

I needed everyone on side, for they were my lifeblood, which could snuff me out with betrayal whenever they wished. They never did. They were the ones who benefited after all and would not cut off their nose to spite their face.

My only problem was the gentry. Most were involved in smuggling operations. Some even financed it; such as my relationship with John Tonkin and the Arundell's.

But the likes of George Borlace, Walter Borlace, the Godolphin's and their heirs, would hound me to this very day.

That is why I needed a friend as powerful as Lord Arundell.

My wealth had grown from strength to strength with his patronage. But when John Tonkin found me in the Turks head in Penzance one night shortly after the Dutch wreck, I had to be straight with him to ensure it stayed that way. He would have found out sooner or later that I had salvaged cargo from the wrecked ship. He was far too well connected to not have known.

'Ah… I have been looking for you Mr Carter; dreadfully sorry to hear about your father by the way.' It was kind of him to say so, and I was not surprised he knew about it. I had to talk fast, before he could ask the question I knew he would ask. 'Thank you, Mr Tonkin, he is at peace I suppose. But let us talk of merrier tidings. Like the goods I have salvaged for Lord Arundell from the Dutch wreck,' I said, and clinked my cup to his conspiringly. He smiled and raised both of his leather gloved hands together, as if pleasantly surprised by my news. But he knew; and played his ignorance well.

'That's wonderful John… wonderful. How much did you salvage?' he asked.

'Most of it; you will be pleased to hear. I have used some to pay the lads for transport, and I'm assuming Lord Arundell and yourself will desire me to distribute it.' He could see where I was going, and winked at me, laughing at my blatant efforts to gain favour, at the same time as earning a share of the booty.

'Yes of course John… that would be most agreeable indeed. Shall we say forty percent of the profits?' That was generous indeed. I had played an honest hand yet again, and God had seen me right, through his instrument Mr Tonkin. The rest of the profit would be split between him and Lord Arundell.

If I hadn't cut them in, I would have made a fortune. But I would have also lost the trust and future profit from the man sat before me, and I could not let that happen.

'You are a rare one you know John Carter.' He pulled a pipe and searched his pockets for tobacco.

I had been hoping he would do that, and I threw a small oilskin of the stuff on the table. His hat flew over the top of it, realizing what it was quickly. 'That's for you personally Mr Tonkin,' I said, and toasted him once again. I had told my partner James of my offering, and he thought I was mad. He never could see the big picture. It was just as well he had a Carter as a partner.

'Thank you for that; I knew you would be a tremendous asset to us. Let's say that after you have settled your recent acquisitions, we go and buy a lager cargo. Fully financed our end of course; my agent will be ready with the cargo at Guernsey when you are ready.'

I had hoped he would say that.

We are a speculating family us Carter's, and my dreams were as deep as the ocean. 'How soon can he be ready with the cargo?' I asked interested.

'Well…he could be ready in a few weeks I suppose. But you will surly need longer to distribute what you have currently.'

Now I was the one smiling. 'Actually John,' I said, daring to call him by his Christian name. 'That pouch of tobacco was the last of the goods we had. The rest is gone and sold,' I said, and slid a chest of coin I'd been keeping under the table with the finest pair of leather boot I've ever owned.

This was to be my grand presentation to impress him and take me seriously enough to invest in me for the foreseeable future.

'That is your sixty percent sir.' I reverted to address him formally. He looked at me wide eyed. 'This is unbelievable man,' he said in surprised shock at the amount of money which had been below us the whole time. 'I think I owe you a drink John Carter.' That night he introduced me to his many wealthy friends, and for the first time in my life, I had rubbed shoulders with real gentlemen of note. Their cloth was finer than mine, but I did not look out of place among them. We drank and spoke of enterprise and wealth creation all night. I conversed at length with them, and he introduced me as his young prodigy and business partner.

I don't think I bought a drink all night, and they had all welcomed me as an equal.

My new wealth and forty percent cut, which I had already presumed to keep, was buried inside a cave not far from Cuddan Point.

With the amount of money I gave John Tonkin, I knew he would not even question my forty percent. But judging by the weight of his chest, he would know I had made a very tidy sum. I was going from leaps and bounds.

Before I finally left their good company, I said a silent prayer to God, who I felt was watching over me in that moment of triumph.

CHAPTER 9

I was riding high and climbing the ladder of success with uncommon swiftness. I must sound immodest as you read this, but it was all true.

When I think back to those early years, I can't believe I was accepted so readily by my peers and the locality.

I look at young lads today, which further amazes me for what I had achieved so quickly. My brothers shared my talent for commerce, Harry being the prime example in later years. But his tale will come later in my story; and what a life that man led I can tell you.

Things for me early on as I have said, came easily. I recognised the money and wealth a man could earn from smuggling. It was not surprising considering the ridicules amount of tax being levied on the many imported items we brought in.

Before my time, the government tried to lower the tax on tea. This was an economic solution to stop smuggling at its roots. But smugglers just turned to other items, such as spirits and silk to counter this move by the government. Subsequently, tea duties were raised again and the good times for bringing in contraband continued.

I would purchase everything I could get my hands on. The two sloops we had were in constant action, and James and I were doing very nicely for ourselves indeed.

It was the year of our Lord 1756 when the good times started to go sour. Hostilities with France had turned into all-out war. In America we fought them for land, and it was only a matter of time before war would spread across Europe, nay even the whole known world.

My hero, King Fredrick II of Prussia was making grand moves on the continent as well. Austria had made the attempt to retake the rich province of Silesia, which he had taken from them in the 1740s. The attempt to take it back failed and Austria were poised to make a massive incursion into Prussia itself.

King Fredrick however was not called the Great for nothing, and always liked to attack first. And attack he did.

He and his forces marched into Saxony and occupied its capital Dresden, thus cutting of the Saxon forces from its Austrian allies. The Austrians who needed allies naturally turned to their old enemy France, who were allied to Russia causing an axis against the surrounded Fredrick.

He was then forced to fight on several fronts and beat back each aggressor systematically. Even Sweden became involved, further bolstering the Austrian forces against Prussia. Some called it luck on the part of Fredrick, to come out of the conflict as greatly as he did. I however, could see the skill involved, and I emulated myself on his tactics of mobility and aggression, to take out an enemy piece by piece. He had been outnumbered and outgunned, but he turned his weakness into his strength by out manoeuvring his enemies in a masterful military campaign.

Britain incidentally, had allied itself to Prussia, and the conflict affected everything, including trade and taxation. But when other smugglers saw unacceptable risk when putting to sea in those troubled times. I like the King of Prussia saw opportunity; and like him, would use my weaknesses as strengths. Perhaps I was foolish in my youth; reckless maybe.

I could only see the upside of higher taxation and war; which were massive profits.

The crown had to pay for the soldiers somehow, so they filled the war chest with taxation. They also allowed privateering, which became very lucrative for me later.

Privateering was like a form of legalised piracy, and an excellent opportunity for a smuggler to excuse what contraband he had on board, if questioned by the revenue men.

I applied for my letters of marquee, as did many a smuggler. But I was turned down with no thanks to the new Mayor of Penzance, who had heard of my antics, and deplored smuggling with a passion. He was none other than Walter Borlace.

The Onslow-Borlace family were influential landowners and made it their duty to extent that influence in any position of office they could get their hands on. They were also enemies of the Arundell's, and anyone else who enjoyed their patronage. Unfortunately, this included me, and I beseeched John Tonkin to do what he could to get me my papers to privateer.

Alas; he could not change the minds of the admiralty, who had already read the damning letter of my character by Mayor and Magistrate Walter Borlace. The good times and smooth sailing were about to get choppy for me.

But sometimes the harder paths we take are the most character building. For me, this would prove true.

'I can't believe we've been turned down. What more can we do to carry favour at the Admiralty?' I said frustrated to John Tonkin, who shook his head in equal frustration.

He had tried to pull some strings to get me those letters to privateer, which would have benefited him enormously.

'Walter Borlace has played his hand well, dam him. I have tried everything. You are still young though John. The war with France will last many years yet lad,' he said to me, trying to raise my spirits.

'Let's just forget it and look to fill our pockets, eh?' he added, knowing that talk of business would always get me excited. It was safe to say that over those two years, I had become good friends with John Tonkin. He had been a kind of mentor to me and I will always be grateful for it. The contacts and introductions he gave me were priceless. And he made me his project, to which I kindly accepted graciously.

It was not all one way I might add. I was making him a fortune with my contacts among the common man; previously inaccessible to a man of the gentry. I had introduced him to the Vingoe family, and so our network of partners grew, and became as organised as any military campaign.

'The prices at Guernsey have crept up somewhat,' I said. The war had pushed up prices in everything, and the French were feeling the pinch just as we were.

'I have two cargos bound from France, and they're willing to meet us at sea just off the coast of Guernsey. Are you up for going John?'

I was up for anything, and in my arrogance, I accepted to meet the French crews. I was a cocky, strapping young man, and first officer of a small cutter, which I owned outright, along with four sloops I had running contraband in and out of Porthleah.

That place was now becoming known as Kings Cove, because of people comparing me to the mighty King Fredrick.

I added fuel to this legend of course, further enhancing my reputation as an up and coming man within the profession.

'You know I'll do it,' I said.

And off I went to collect our cheap gin and brandy from our French partners. For us, the war was with the politicians and kings. When all was said and done, trade needed to continue for our survival.

***

My small cutter was named Agnes after my mother, and she was captained by my friend William Vingoe, who'd become a master sailor and smuggler in his own right. My cousin Henry and my partner James were also on board, making my cutter formidable in the hands of their expertise.

I hope I'm not selling myself short by saying that I was good at sea.

My expertise was with people and making deals.

Sailing, navigation and all the many things a seaman must know, such as tides were all necessary to learn to become the king of smuggling.

However; I knew talent when I saw it, and the crew with me on my cutter, although young, were second to none at the time.

This would be one of my golden rules of success; surround yourself with excellence, and then let their light shine on you.

We knew we were good too. The customs men did not stand a chance against our expertise, and we outran them on countless occasions.

Going to meet the French for our cargo seemed like the easiest thing in the world to me and my crew of twelve lads.

The weather that day was cold and blustery. A light rain came down persistently, until we were all completely wet through.

Even my great leather overcoat failed to keep the rain at bay.

You would think that we would curse such a day, for who would want to put to sea in such conditions. That was exactly why we rejoiced when the sea was so unwelcoming. There would be few others out on the water today, and that meant the coast was clear as we used to say.

As we set out from Penzance harbour, most folk were tucked up and warm in their houses, or inside a tavern with a fire and warm meal on their table. But just as we weighed anchor, I could see a man wave out to a fast-looking sloop, which then set sail before us.

My eyesight has always been good, and I noticed the man waving on shore was none other than the Ferret Ferris, who I had not seen for a long time. Every now and then we would bump into one another and trade insults, but we had not come to blows again since my father's funeral a few years before. It was curious why he was here, and waving out to the sloop, which had sailed out of sight.

Whenever I saw the Ferret, I thought he would try and get revenge for the beating I had given him.

But once at sea I did not think anything more of it, and later that day we were at the meeting spot, just off the coast of Guernsey waiting for our cargo to arrive. We were to look out for two sloops, sailing together hoisting blue flags. We were flying red flags, and once we found one another, we would load the barrels from their boat to ours accordingly.

We did not have to wait long for their arrival, and when they came, they shouted over in broken English, that they could not unload at sea with the dire weather and crashing waves. They said they had dumped the cargo on the French coast not far from St-Malo.

I was not happy about it at all, considering the risk involved. My cousin Henry also protested, but he did about most things, and was ignored.

It had been William Vingoe, always the most daring of us bar me, that calmed everyone's nerves.

'I know that part of the coast well John,' he said to me confidently. 'It will be fine. No one will be around anyway in this weather.' He was the Captain of the cutter, but I owned it; and my say would be final. Even my partner James would defer to me for approval on matters of importance. He had learned I could make decisions under pressure, and I always came out smelling of roses.

'I haven't come all this way just to catch pneumonia. Follow them William. Just keep your eye out for treachery,' I said making my mind up.

The coastline of France was well known to me thanks to the tutelage of William, James and Henry, who all spoke French quite well.

As we swung our cutter along the barren coastline, you could have been fooled into thinking that you were sailing along the counties of England, and we dropped anchor near some caves not so dissimilar to own ones back at Prussia Cove. We had four carriage guns, and two swivel guns at port and starboard, which would deter even the most determined of customs men, or anyone else who fancied their chances against our interests.

Eventually we found the spot where the Frenchmen had stored our cargo, and we wasted no time at all in bringing it on board.

When it was stowed safely away, the lads and I calmed ourselves and relaxed with no thought of anything but our profits.

That was a huge mistake, and while I kicked away some rats that scurried below deck around our barrels, I heard a loud bang from above.

My confident swagger and untouchable ego was crushed down to size in an instant. I heard shots fired, and rain coming down in sheets, gushing through the holes and gaps in the deck above. I could just make out shouting voices in French, followed by the familiar retort by William in the same language.

I pocked my head above deck to see it was swarming with French soldiers, all with murderous looks on their faces. They carried muskets with bayonets attached, as the gunpowder would have been so soaked, making them all useless now. The shot I had heard was probably a warning, from a musket covered from the rain.

I had achieved so much, in such a short space of time, I thought myself untouchable. When a man faces his death, he will do two things; fight or flight. Looking at the rain dripping off the end of the bayonets, would have sent many a man overboard to take his chances on land. I could not let all that I had worked for be snuffed out by my own lack of vigilance. So naturally I decided what the obvious course of action should be. I would fight.

I came out of my hiding place like a banshee from hell, screeching insanely to try and panic our boarders. But I had not seen the foe that loomed over the hatch, who struck me over the head with what felt like a cannon ball. The cannon ball was in fact a cudgel which knocked me senseless. Then darkness came, and for all I knew, I had been killed were I stood.

CHAPTER 10

I awoke groggily, feeling straw around my fingertips, and quickly placed my hand on an egg sized lump forming at the back of my head. The blow had been hard enough to split my skin, and blood had clotted around the wound in a sticky mess of congealed hair. It was dark and cold, and I stood to trace the walls of my environment. I was in a prison cell.

I tripped over a body on the floor and heard a grunt below me. 'Who's there?' I demanded. 'Where am I?' The body I had tripped on had gotten to his feet, and I backed away from the outline, not wishing anymore harm to befall my already fragile state.

'John, it's me; for a moment there I thought they'd killed you.' To my relief it was the recognisable voice of William Vingoe. 'What happened?' I asked him, sliding down the cool damp wall to rest my shaking legs.

'They came out of nowhere John. One minute I was watching the beach, then suddenly they fired their cannon, and men were climbing on board in a flash,' he said sullenly.

The King of Prussia Cove

'Are you alright? Did we lose any men?' I asked concerned about the welfare of my good friends, who may well all be dead.

'I'm fine; no more than a few bruises. The others seemed well too before we were separated. Unfortunately, the cargo has all been taken, along with the sloop,' William said dismayed.

The loss would cost us a large sum of money, and I kicked myself for allowing the French soldiers to take us so easily. The damp in the prison had a musty odour, and the straw under our feet smelled like it'd been a bed for pigs. It was rank; and I curled my nose up in disgust. Once coming to my senses fully, William and I discussed at length what had happened.

Apparently, the French smugglers had been in on the deception, and we had walked right into their trap, hook line and sinker. They would be rubbing their hands together, for the coin we had to purchase the contraband was considerable. That and my boat were now their property.

This was soon confirmed by our captors, who came to our cell in the early hours of the morning.

'Hello, my friends; my name is Lieutenant Domenici, and you are now prisoners of war,' he announced to us in accented English, looking quite pleased with himself at the gullible enemy now in his custody

'That may be so. But we are not soldier's sir. We are but humble fisherman, lured into a trap by your countryman,' I said as calmly as I could. He just smiled, and put his hands on his forehead, seeming to have made a terrible mistake.

'Oh... my apologies; if you are not soldiers, then that must make you spies? That is unfortunate my friends. We shoot spies in France,' he threatened, as if the matter had been resolved.

'You know dam well we're not spies!' William said sternly to the Lieutenant. Our captor's eyebrows rose in mock consideration of what we had said. He knew we were not spies, but we would be mouths to feed and shelter, and that he could do without. A firing squad could remedy that problem very rapidly for him.

Something had to be done, and fast. I was angry at our predicament, but anger and rage would be useless if we wanted to survive.

Instead I would need to use guile, cunning, and charm. I reached for a hidden pocket inside my great coat, which I still wore gratefully. To my relief the two gold coins that I had been keeping for an emergency such as this, were safe and sound.

He could have just taken them from me of course. But I learned very early, that if you give a man a gift in such a way, he often feels obliged enough to look upon you favourably. Most men would anyway. There was always the odd one or two that were incorruptible. Or wicked enough to take your gift and kill you without a second thought.

Options unfortunately were few, and I played my hand the only way I knew how.

'You must excuse my hot-headed friend sir. He is understandably distressed; as am I. What he tells you however is true. We are not spies. I tell you this on our honour and before God. You have done very well from us today sir, and I congratulate you for your efforts. We were plainly outclassed by your military skill, and you are probably thinking that getting rid of us would be the easiest thing to do now.'

He had a well-groomed moustache that half twitched with amusement. 'Yes. That would be the easiest thing, would it not?' he agreed still smiling.

'I would like to offer you another alternative sir.' And like a magician, I produced the gold coins that I held into a small ray of light beaming through the cells only barred window. The sleight of hand was impressive, and he nodded his head appreciatively. 'Go on,' he prompted me.

'I would like to buy my freedom with this sir, if I may.'

'I could just take that from you now, and still shoot you,' he replied.

That was true; he could have done that.

But I had been prepared for that response. So, with my head pounding with pain, I made the deal of my life, nay for my life.

'You could do that. That is true. But I have a thousand pounds, which says you will not.' I said, and let my words hang in the air like bait for a greedy fish.

And just like a fish, he started to nibble.

'What thousand pounds could you give me?' he said interested, yet with a hint of scepticism in his voice. He had enjoyed seeing me pull the coins, and now he looked at me expecting me to pull out my new offer from thin air.

Like any good performer I kept his anticipation in check long enough to enjoy my every word.

I poured the gold coins theatrically into his hand, dropping them from high so he would have to catch them. 'I have a chest of coin buried in a cave back home. Let me go and fetch it back to buy our freedom.' I said calmly.

'Ha… you must think I am stupid Englishman. If I let you go, you will be gone. I would not blame you for it. Your friends might be upset though,' he said convinced I would betray my crew for my own freedom.

'I do not ask to go sir. I have a partner who you have here I presume; he also knows the location of the chest. Let him go and fetch it back to you for our freedom. What have you got to lose by releasing one of us? The reward on the other hand would be considerable,' I reasoned in a last-ditch attempt to sway him.

'What is the name of your crewman who knows of this chest of money?' he asked evenly. He did not have to get animated for me to know in that moment that he had taken my bait.

'James Thomas sir; all he would need is a boat with a sail to get across the channel.' He looked at me pensively, before turning and leaving the cell abruptly. My heart sank, as I assumed he had changed his mind. Instead he looked though the bars examining us like animals.

'I will think about your offer English,' he concluded finally, and left us to sit in the stinking straw.

William just stared at me open mouthed and shook his head in amazement.

'If we die together and end up at the gates of hell John. Will you speak for me?'

We both laughed, and I hoped my words had indeed struck home. We were not out of danger just yet. We had to wait for our answer, and salvation to come.

***

The next day we were all put together in a larger cell, and that was a blessing to see our crew alive and well.

I had been the only casualty, and the lump on my head had felt like it would hit the ceiling. It was enormous, and still very painful. But I hid my discomfort from the lads, whose spirits rose upon our reunion.

The mood didn't last long though, when William and I told them about the threat of a firing squad. I calmed them down and explained that I had tried to cut a deal with our gaoler, Lieutenant Domenici.

I expressed to James his part to play. 'I need you to go to our cave and bring it all. That's if he goes for it. I'm almost certain he will.'

James didn't hesitate to agree, and I knew he would return if we got the chance. There are rare things in this world, and good friends are perhaps the rarest of all. I was lucky to have such good friends.

'You want me to bring it all John?' he asked me after I had gone over what he must do in detail.

'Yes. Bring it all, I have an idea, and if things go according to how I think they will go, then this disaster could be salvaged somewhat,' I said to him where we stood in a corner of the cell.

Unfortunately, days went by, then weeks. I thought with much fear that I had failed to tempt the Lieutenant with the promise of my fortune.

The lads were certain we would be executed, and they could very well have been right. William had managed to talk to a gaoler who'd brought us dry bread and murky looking water. He was a

The King of Prussia Cove

simpleton really, but we found out from him that we were not far from St-Malo, in a prison of war at a town called Dinan. The castle we were being kept in housed all manner of rouges, including captured sailors and soldiers.

We kept up moral by singing loud and merrily, long into the night. That drove our gaolers mad, and they would bang on the bars with clubs to frighten us into silence. The dim-witted gaoler seemed to enjoy our shanties though, and he would hum along to the English words that he surly could not understand.

After about a month or so I was taken, along with James and William by an entourage of guards. We were taken across the courtyard and led up a tower to a room. It was pleasingly warm inside from an open fire, which crackled on the other side. It probably wasn't that hot to be honest, but we had been cold and damp for ages, and the warmth caressed our skin with much needed comfort. I lavished every second we had in that room.

Sitting at a large oak table was none other than Lieutenant Domenici, who was enjoying a glass of claret and smoking a pipe while he examined us without a word. We stood there in silence, and I nodded to him in greeting. He did not respond, and just continued to gaze, at me.

The fire spat, and suddenly he asked the other guards to leave the room. We were all in iron shackles anyway, so could do him no harm, nor cause any mischief. I did note that there were three chairs on the other side of the table. 'Sabastian, could you bring up some food,' he said to the last guard to leave. 'I take it you are hungry?' We all nodded vigorously to his obvious question. 'We are very hungry sir; not that we are not being treated fairly that is, but I won't lie to you, I could eat a horse.' He inclined his head to acknowledge me at last.

'I could have that arranged for you, but horse is not on the menu today,' he told me amused.

I knew they ate horses in France, and I had been telling the truth when I could have eaten a whole one.

Instead he got straight to the point, and put down his pipe, and pulled out some paper, ink and quill.

He would either be giving us our death sentences or handing us a lifeline. I was sure he could hear my beating heart, which pounded once more in anticipated dread. 'Now, Mr...?'

'Carter...John Carter sir,' I replied trying to keep the fear from my voice, and that was proving difficult. I held my breath and he continued, not seeming to notice our anxiety.

'I have thought about your offer at great length John Carter. Unfortunately, my superiors will demand that you be held or shot. Otherwise they will know something suspicious has occurred,' he said as a matter of fact to us. The weight of my doom was descending upon me, but I did not think that talking was the best idea, so stayed silent and nodded my understanding.

'That is not to say we cannot get around this... problem,' he added, offering us a glimmer of hope, which blew the blessed wind back into my sails.

'There is always a way sir. I would love to hear your proposal,' I said with confidence returning to me. I could now negotiate as I would with any other person. I just had to know if he had been interested to renew the bartering.

'I am sure you would Mr Carter. Your offer of a thousand pounds seems very generous; I would like to accept your deal under one condition.' He began to write on the paper with a flourish.

'Name your condition,' I said, making out that I had a choice in the matter.

'One of my men will accompany your man to England, to ensure his return. If he comes back with the full amount, then you may all leave here in some way or form,' he said.

'What does that mean?' William asked suspiciously. 'Does some shape or form mean alive sir?' he enquired stiffly.

William was not the most skilled at negotiations. But his tactical mind served him well at sea, where he was a master of his profession. Like any cut and thrust with an enemy, he was sniffing out whether this was another trap.

'Well... we cannot let you just walk out of this castle, even if you do meet your end of the bargain. But I have a plan that will suit us all. Basically, we will line you up against the wall with powdered muskets and shoot at you without the shot being rammed. You simply play dead and we send you on your way under the cover of night. My superior will not even be there to see it. But he will hear the shots,' he said to us quite pleased with his scheme.

'What about the men firing at us. Will they know what's happening, or will they accidently load a few rounds in the barrel by mistake?' William asked, making his own doubts known clearly. As I sat there at the time, I just wanted him to keep his mouth shut, and leave the negotiations to me. There was another side of me however that wanted to hear the reassurances the Lieutenant could give us.

'The firing at you will be paid from the thousand pounds you will bring. They will get a few coins for the deception. If by chance you do not bring the sum agreed. Well… Those muskets gentlemen will all be firing live rounds. Do you understand?' he announced with menace, letting us know that if we betrayed him, we would all die.

'Yes. I'm sure we all get the picture sir. I can assure you, James will honour our agreement. Wont you James?' I said to my partner, who had been quiet up until now.

'I will bring the chest, make no mistake about that. I must ask sir; will my companion speak good English?' James inquired sheepishly.

'Yes, very good English. Why do you ask?' wondered Domenici, not seeing why it mattered.

'It's just that… we have patrols, just like you do here sir. I don't want to get out of this place only to be hung as a spy in my own country with your man,' James said, and had a very good point too.

'Ah… Yes. My man is fluent, with little to no accent. He will be delivering letters to my agent in your country. That is another reason why I send him, as well as chaperoning you on your voyage.' the Lieutenant explained to my much-relaxed partner. I wondered who his agent in England was, but I would not dare to presume to ask such a foolish question.

After a short time going over the details, we all signed the unofficial agreement, which he also signed and hid under his tunic.

He could have just given us his word. The signed papers did make me happier though. It was more formal; like a business arrangement. I had a feeling that Lieutenant Domenici was a man of commerce. Time would tell whether my assumption would be proved correct.

CHAPTER 11

It took a few more weeks to make the arrangements for James to leave us and pick up the chest for our French hosts. After our little meeting with Lieutenant Domenici, our conditions improved slightly, and we were given better food to eat, and sometimes even a bit of grog to wash it down. He would send for me and William some evenings and would ask us endless questions about the smuggling profession, to which we were both experts in its intricacies.

He wanted to know what fetched the highest price, and how much a man could earn from doing it. The simple answer was a great deal of money. But you had to know what you were doing to avoid the authorities who would harass and hound us from land and sea.

We told him about the riding officers, roving in packs up and down the coast, poking their noses into every inn and township to end the smuggling man.

His curiosity was born out of greed of course. It was understandable seeing us young lads with a thousand pounds at our

The King of Prussia Cove

disposal. After many such candle lit meetings, we started to become friendly with the Lieutenant, and a few days before James was due to leave with his agent, I asked him a question that had been on my mind for a while.

'How did you know we were coming Lieutenant? Our meet was arranged by a gentleman with the upmost discretion on our end.' I poured some claret from a jug he had graciously shared with us. 'The agent meeting our man in England is from Cornwall, such as you are. He sent word to us that a smuggling vessel, lightly armed, were on their way to collect goods from France. The men you were dealing with at Guernsey did not have a choice other than to betray you,' he said, and guzzled down the wine I had poured him.

'So, you knew all along we were smuggling men and not spies.' I stated with a half smirk, keeping the mood light. We were friendly, but I wanted to keep it that way.

'Yes. I knew who you were. But it is our duty to apprehend such craft for the glory of France you see.'

For the glory of his purse more than likely I thought. I did not tell him that, but it was obvious.

'What's the name of your man over in England? I might know him,' I asked, probably pushing my luck somewhat. I had an idea who it could be. If I ever got myself out of the mess, I would dig a little deeper to confront our betrayer. 'I cannot tell you that Mr Carter. Secrecy is everything. There is a war on you know.' I had not expected him to answer me, and later when I returned to our cell, I had a few more instructions to give to James before he left for home.

The rest of the lads were just nodding off on our freshly laid straw beds all around our feet. We whispered so no one would wake or over hear our discussion.

'When you get back, watch out and take note of who the French contact is. I have a funny feeling we may know him,' I said, trying to keep my voice down.

'I will John; who do you think it was that sent them word?'

'I think it was my old friend The Ferret. Do you remember he waved off that sloop, right before we left? I don't think it was personal against me. I just think he spies for them. If it's true, make sure you hide your face, or he could stir more treachery. You know what he's like.'

There was something else I wanted him to do, and he had a say whether to agree or disagree, seeing that we were partners.

'One last thing; I think our new friend the Lieutenant will be a valuable ally if we pull this off, so I want you to do something for us. It's risky but could be highly rewarding.' I went over my plan, and it took a long time arguing with him in whispers to get my point across. Eventually, he agreed to do what I asked him, still with reluctance, though not enough to have me worried if he would complete the task or not.

***

Like watching a pot of water boil, we waited impatiently for his return and our liberation. One week went by, then two.

I was becoming worried as were the lads, whose dirty and dishevelled appearances suited our surroundings within our temporary home at Dinan Castle.

From my cell window I could see the river traffic coming and going, and I hoped every day to see James return.

But still we waited.

One morning about three weeks after his departure, we were woken by the simpleton gaoler, who called for me to go with him immediately.

At the time, I had assumed our time was up, and they were sick of my grand lies enough to shoot us to a man. As usual, I was led across the court yard, and found myself once again in the presence of the Lieutenant, who was standing by the table in his quarters, beaming a grin ear to ear. I then praised God. For the man standing with him, was my friend James Thomas, in spanking fresh cloths.

I noticed my strong box on the table, and I hoped it was full of the money I had promised. It would be hard to part with it. I could have bought land with that amount, or more luggers to bring in more wealth. I had earned every penny in that chest. But without our lives, it was all worthless.

I would earn it all back, and much more I told myself.

As the Lieutenant opened the chest and put his fingers through the coins like a man would stroke his wife, I made my move, deciding I had the measure of him.

'Our part of the bargain is honoured now sir. Will you now honour yours?' Domenici turned to look at me, but I could tell he wanted to look back at his new-found wealth, which he did as he answered.

'There will be no rounds of shot available to my firing squad Mr Carter.' He turned again to shut the chests lid, while James came and placed what I had asked from him in my hand, making it look like a greeting, or a friendly handshake.

He stepped outside leaving me alone with the Lieutenant. 'You know this could be, only the beginning Lieutenant. You are a man of opportunity, just as I am. I realise that I am still your prisoner sir, but I feel we have become friends due to our mutual interests. Please stop me if my assumptions are incorrect.'

'No, no… you are an intriguing character, and I would dare say I now know you to be a man of your word. I could count you a friend, though our countries are technically at war,' he said in his cultured French accent.

'The war won't last forever you know, and a man must still make a living. Let me ask you sir, what if I was to propose a partnership of sorts, an arrangement. I buy the goods directly from you, instead of our usual supplier. The thousand pounds here will seem like a paltry sum, compared to the riches which can be made in smuggling into Briton. In return I can bring you Cornish wool, a produce of much worth in your country I understand.'

I let him think about the opportunity for a moment. For all I knew he would change his mind, keep the money anyway and still shoot us all.

He nodded slowly. I could sense his pleasure at the cheek of the young lad before him, offering him wealth way beyond what a soldier could ever earn legitimately. He had some money I understood later. But being the youngest son in a middle-class family had forced him to make his own way in the world.

'You wish to trade with me after the war?' he asked me and gestured for me to sit at the table with him.

'Why wait?' I said, energetically. 'There is no treason at play if they don't find out. The price for brandy and other contraband has gone up to impossible heights because of the war. That's why we tried to buy from France in the first place. The margin of profit to be gained would make us rich men. And when the war is over, we can live like kings, or continue our arrangement even further. What do you say man?'

My eagerness was infectious, and he was becoming just as animated as I was. He scratched his hairline were his less than expensive wig had chaffed him. In his mind, the money he could make with me could attire him with the finest wigs, powders and cloth a man could buy.

'I am interested indeed Mr Carter. I could be executed for making such an arrangement. But I am a speculating man, with high ambitions. I think I could work with you sir. When would you like to begin trading?' he asked, and walked to a cabinet for some cups, so we could toast our deal over some wine. As he brought our drinks, I threw a purse onto the table theatrical as usual. I loved adding drama to a deal. They loved it too, thinking they were getting treated with special care.

'I would like to begin dealing with you immediately sir,' I offered with gusto.

'In that purse is the amount I had to purchase my last cargo, which was commandeered by your government. I asked James to bring it to me, and it is now all the wealth I have. I offer this to you now as payment for the brandy and claret that I presume you now have stored under the castle. I will also need my ship of course to transport it back. This sir, can be the first of many such deals.'

I was pushing my luck, but in my experience if you didn't ask you didn't get. I had wooed him with riches untold. I had sold my dream of adventurous profiteering, and in those days, for the likes of men like us, the only way to gain wealth such as we did, was to sail against the wind and break some rules.

Yes, we would be risking our lives. But how would the risk be any different from what we had already been doing.

He laughed. Gently at first; then he became louder and louder. It made him look like he had lost his mind. I could not have played my hand any better, and I smiled at him and poured us both more wine. He drank his, trying not to spit any out with his mirth.

Now was the time for me to be silent.

I had seen too many times before, when men talked themselves out of a perfectly reasonable deal, all because they could not keep their mouth shut.

I let him calm down from laughing, and he stared at me over the table, still with a smile on his face, but kept his eyes neutral.

'If you are as good a smuggler as you are at making deals John Carter, then how can I go wrong? I accept. Let us make our fortune.' He reached over the table, just as he did on our last deal for the thousand pounds release money. Only this time, he pumped my hand eagerly. We stayed in his quarters most of that day and into the evening, going over how we would move the contraband from country to country safely. We spoke of logistics, and who we could trust to come on board with us.

I could vouch for my crew and some other lads back home. He told me he had dozens of soldiers and sailors he could rely on his end to make it work.

I was eighteen, and as comfortable at making deals then, as I am now. Deal making, and smuggling went hand in hand you see. There were smugglers everywhere in those days. The ones who became successful, the ones who became legends, all had the same thing in common. They knew how to make good deals.

That is how a man grows a stable empire; and with the new bargain made, it was time to get back to my Kingdom at Prussia Cove and begin my own legend.

CHAPTER 12

Even though we were now going to be released. We still had to wait for a few more months before we were all lined up against a wall in front of a firing squad. Our time up until then had not been completely unpleasant. The food for example improved tremendously after I had paid the money for our freedom.

I was confident that no shot what so ever had been loaded into the guns arrayed before us.

They were military issue Charleville muskets, which had a range of just over one hundred and sixty yards. The accuracy of the weapons was poor to say the least. We stood only twenty yards away and accurate or not, at that range, they would be lethal.

Long before we came out into the courtyard to face our fabricated dooms, I had told the lads how I wanted them to react when the guns went off. The whole thing was supposed to be rehearsed, so we could trick Lieutenant Domenici's commanding officer, who was an elderly Colonel, expecting us all to be shot as spies.

The shooters were in on the deception of course, and I had hoped he paid them well.

Even though the day was cool, I could feel drops of sweat running down my back, as the Sergeant gave the order to take aim. Some of the lads kissed crosses hanging around their necks and said the Lord's Prayer with genuine fear that they would soon very well be meeting their maker.

I had told them my deal, and the need to play along for the benefit of appearances. But I was young, and some of them did not know me well enough to believe in my boast of negotiating freedom for everyone.

I had become nervous at the time as well if I am being truthful.

After all, Domenici had been given a large sum of money and he also had our ship and cargo, which he could resell for more coin.

What if he had just humoured me into some kind of double cross, so I could be led calmly, like a lamb to the slaughter?

I closed my eyes and silently prayed to God with the rest of the men. I like to think our maker always looked out for me and my family. Do not get me wrong, we had been tested on occasion, sometimes with near death consequences. But we would always come out of it clean.

The Sergeant gave the order, and I tensed in anticipation of the shot striking me. The hammers fell, and the flints ignited the powder, deafening our ears with a thunderous crack.

Yet no searing hot shot had touched me. I could have been mistaken, for I had heard once that sometimes the shock of being shot can be quite painless. I dropped to the floor anyway, trusting that all was going to plan, as did the rest of the men.

We were all alive, and had all dramatically faked our demise in unison, as would an actor from the famous theatres of London. We all held little bottle of pig's blood that we poured onto our chests as we played our deathly parts. It was just as well the commanding officer had not been present for our performance. I am sure my acting was as grand as I felt it had been at the time. But when I snuck a peak at the firing squad, from where I lay on the hay covered floor. I watched them laugh to the point of tears falling down their cheeks.

That was when another thought had come to me. Perhaps we were never going to be executed, and the laughter at our theatrics had all been just a practical joke. If that was true, then I would have commended him on making prize fools out of us.

I did ask him many years later if this was the case. He just smiled and denied it profusely. I still have my suspicions today. An old man such as me gets to muse on the many adventures I've had in my youth.

And I had memory of many more near death experiences to come after that. I am still having them actually. I love adventures even though I am an old codger.

***

After we were taken to my cutter, which had been fully loaded with French spirits; we all rejoiced once more at our good fortune. The carriage guns on deck had been removed, but I had expected that. They couldn't let a ship laden with French goods and bound for England, leave with a full complement of weapons.

The fresh sea air blew through our sails helping our swift and welcomed departure. We had been gone for nearly a year, with no word of our welfare to reassure family and friends.

Most folk believed our crew lost to sea or killed by pirates or the French. The later had nearly been the case.

Oh, what joy we had when we returned to Prussia Cove, which it was becoming known then, and still is today. It was also known as Kings Cove because of my fascination and admiration of the great Fredrick of Prussia.

My welcome back at Bessie's beer house was worthy of any king returning from war in triumph. I had sent word to John Tonkin in Penzance the very day we arrived back. He joined us in the celebrations and marvelled with the rest when I told him our tale of capture, imprisonment and our eventual release, with a cargo of contraband, and our vessel to boot.

'I thought you were dead John,' he said to me in awed astonishment. I told him about our new friend and partner in France, to which he questioned me extensively about. I needed the deep pockets of the Arundell's and John Tonkin to make the whole scheme in France work.

'It's risky John; very risky. We'll be dodging the French at sea, as well as our own authorities.' I nodded in agreement. I had sold him the deal very convincingly, and any further push may have sent him in the wrong direction.

'We could hang for it; or worse.' I applied just a gentle prod at his sense of ambition. One that I knew he shared with me.

'The risk is great, that is true. But the reward, if this works out, will launch us into the realms of success that folks only dream about.'

I may have been exaggerating, but the blunt truth of the matter was, the price of French goods had risen by over seventy percent and was in high demand. Anybody who could get their hands-on contraband while the war was on would make a fortune.

'We are speculating men, are we not sir. I am young, as are you. I know we can make this work if we are diligent and use our wits. What say you?'

He was a natural risk taker, and when the stakes were high, he would normally double down for an even greater reward. I had seen him do it at cards many times.

'Yes… yes we shall. You have done well John. You have created this opportunity. It is only fair that your percentage goes up in kind. You've earned it,' he said to me excited.

My usual cut of forty percent was high indeed, so any increase would be very generous. John Tonkin always rewarded enterprise. I would learn a few tricks off him over time. One of them is that looking after men who looked after you would ensure you prospered.

I waited for him as he worked out my new cut. 'Shall we say an even fifty percent of profits,' he said at last.

Now I was the one who stared astonished at him. 'That would be most agreeable. Thank you,' I replied to him, for the first time lost for words. With the quantities we were planning on buying. Fifty percent would make me an extremely rich man. James came over to the table and landed on a chair next to me. He was well on the way to becoming blind drunk and lost his hat as he toasted the pair of us, exposing his famous ginger curly hair. He had poured most of the ale he was about to drink down his waistcoat.

We discussed our financing arrangements with him, but he normally left those complexities to me. He would not question or remember the fine details in the morning. But he was always paid his fair share. He would also be a man of considerable means if things worked out.

Before he eventually fell asleep on the table, we turned our discussion to more serious matters.

'While we were held John, we discovered who betrayed our rendezvous for the original cargo. James managed to spot him on his return to England with his French escort,' I said, trying to keep the anger from my voice. The man who had betrayed us to the French had very nearly got us killed.

'Who is it man!' John Tonkin asked intrigued.

'It was the same man incidentally who sent my father down the mine, and to his death. The same man I lay a beating on. And no surprise, he has looked for revenge ever since. But it seems his hatred for me has led him into betraying his country.'

'I remember you telling me about him; Ferris is it not?'

'It is. Arthur Ferris, the Ferret as we call him.'

'I have heard the name. I do believe he has become a riding officer for our beloved customs men. A place well suited for a traitor I would warrant. Well placed also to line his pockets with confiscated contraband also,' he added in warning. The Ferret would be gunning for me now that I had returned. He may even find out the arrangement which I had made with Lieutenant Domenici and have us on the end of a rope for our efforts.

After all I had been through; I could not let that man spoil everything I had put in place.

'We will need to deal with that man sooner or later,' I said.

'Leave that to me John. I still have some influence to pin

something on him. I will talk to Lord Arundell to see if he can help us.'

In the background a fiddler began to play a merry song, and another pulled out a flute to join in the music. Folk banged on tables in tune to the well-known song. A few lads pulled up the odd wench to dance with them. The fire roared as someone added a few logs to its dying flame casting the place in a nostalgic glow that warmed more than our bodies. It warmed my heart to be back home and among friends again. John Tonkin made his way home, trusting his horse to find its way back. The few remaining at Bessie's place revelled into the small hours of the morning with the music lifting our souls.

As was normal with drunken musicians, the later the hour, the more their music would become melancholic or some would even call romantic if you liked that kind of music.

I was sitting with a few lads, not saying much, but just enjoying the atmosphere, when I had a firm tap on my shoulder, causing me a moment of alarm with its ferocity. I turned and was taken aback by who stood before me.

'Marie...' I said spellbound by the beauty that I had not seen for nearly a year. She was seventeen the last time I had seen her, and she had been a slip of a girl with looks that would drive the local lads mad for a want to converse with the daughter of the Bessie. She had filled out with a curvaceous figure, combined with her pretty features, left me looking at her like a man turned to stone. Her eyes were as blue as the ocean, and they were wells I could have become lost in forever. They were almost feline in shape, making her look cruel or tempting, according to her mood.

The look she had given me defiantly fell into the cruel category. 'John Carter, you've been gone nearly a year, and I you haven't had the decency to even come and talk to me, let alone ask me to dance,' she said to me bitterly, and turned away in annoyance, making her lustrous blond hair sway as she tried to leave. We had been sweet on each other in the past, a fact that most lads my age were jealous about. But we had never really been serious and had only exchanged drunken kisses and boyish flattery. Perhaps she did not see it that way.

Looking at the woman she had become, spurned me into instant action, and I jumped out of my seat to stop her from escaping me. I hoped this was what she had intended, and as I gently caught her arm, feeling her turn without pulling, I knew she had wanted me.

'I… I'm sorry Marie. How could I have missed you?' I said to her stuttering. I was normally so cock sure of myself. I could bargain with peers twice my age and experience. But when I saw Marie after my time away, I was like a fool searching for words. Fortunately, the music picked up and she pulled me into her, and we danced with the rest of the couples.

'You've got bigger John,' she said, as we twirled around the tavern gracefully to the melody. She was correct in that fact. I had grown to my full height of six foot three inches, which was tall compared to most folk around Cornwall. I had lost count of the times that I had banged my head on a low ceiling beam or doorway.

'I like it,' she added coyly, bringing a hand down and around the small of my back. She was so much smaller than me, coming only to the top of my chest.

I picked her up suddenly and twirled her around easily. Perhaps I wanted to show off how powerful I had become from lifting loads of contraband around. She loved it and squealed with delighted pleasure.

I put her down, and for a moment we just stopped and stared at each other. Time seemed to freeze, and the music and all other noise dulled into silence. Her full lips pouted, and she leaned her head back ever so slightly, waiting for me to kiss her. I prolonged that moment for as long as I could. She was beyond beautiful. To this day I have never seen her like in another. Her mother Bessie had been a rare vision in her day. She was an attractive woman herself for her age. But Marie was in her prime, and dancing with me, despite the many men who had attempted to gain her favour.

Then like lightning striking, I claimed my kiss from her, and our lips met moistly and tenderly. She tasted of sweet honey, and I pulled her in tight to me, hearing whoops of encouragement from the lads in the beer house. I did not look up out of embarrassment. I wanted the moment to last forever.

But like every sunrise and passing dawn, the tranquil kiss had to end, and we both began to dance and laugh long into the night, ending up talking on the cliff face, watching the early morning waves crashing on the rocks. The seagulls cried their morning chorus, and I wrapped a blanket around our shadowed forms. We then turned on each other and made love. I did not care about my sinful behaviour. I did not care for anything apart from my sweet Marie, who nestled up to me longingly. Dear Marie, my first love.

We awoke mid-morning, and I should have felt shame for our sinful behaviour. Being a good Methodist, I went to church as much as I could when on shore.

It was only proper and decent of course, to have physical relations under wedlock. That is what we were taught in the good book, but my sinful night with Marie had felt as natural as breathing. We had always been friends, and sometimes as I have said, had a drunken kiss or two.

I didn't know what had changed in me. She was older by only a year since the last time I saw her. But now, as I walked up the rocky cove from washing my face, it was clear something had changed in me. I looked up to her, still sitting where we had lain, and I rung out the sea water from my long dark hair. It trickled down my back cooling me and refreshing my humours from the previous night's activities.

Reading this, you may truly think that all we did in Cornwall was drink and be merry. You would mostly be correct. Even when we were not in a tavern, we would be stocking its cellars with our grog.

I sat back down next to her, and she dried a small amount of water from me with her petticoat.

'Was last night your first time John?'

'It was,' I said honestly, and with a hint of blush coming to my cheeks.

'Me too; we'd best not mention this to anyone. Mother would probably kill you if she found out; even your charms would not protect you,' she warned, and pulled me in for another kiss. She was right in saying that her mother would be displeased. She was a widow of a former smuggler and was no angel herself. But she had always been highly protective of her most precious Marie.

'I wouldn't dare,' I said, and plucked some grass nervously at the thought of her discovering our frolicking.

'I don't regret what we did though Marie. I have always been fond of you, but last night I don't know what came over me. It felt… natural as such.'

'Oh John, I feel the same, but didn't want to say anything. You'll have to marry me now though,' she said with a mischievous grin; one I couldn't read at all.

'Em… well I…' I would have married her that very morning, but I had not expected her to say such a thing, and she laughed at my confusion.

'I am only teasing you; don't worry.' She stood, shaking her head and rolling her eyes at my open-mouthed paralyses.

'I would marry you though John, if you asked me. But don't be so predictable and do it now. Let us get to know one another first. Properly I mean. Then if you are not scared off by my mother. Ask.'

Relaxing, I held both her hands, kissing them tenderly.

'I will ask,' I said to her with certainty.

'But I will do it when you are not expecting it. Plus, I would have to ask old Bess for permission anyway.' We both chuckled at that. 'She likes you, you know,' she told me.

'I can't imagine why.' I said with false modesty.

'You know why, and it's not because of the gin you bring her. She is amused by you I think. You have always intrigued me as well.'

'Have I now?'

'You're not like the rest of the young lads around here. You're young, yet most folk around these parts know your name. You make every man, woman and child feel special, and they love you for that. I love you for that,' she sat on my lap once more. I never worried too much about what people thought of me. I had ambition, but I also had strict and honest principals. This however proved to give me a reputation as a man a person could trust. Her affection was no less different to theirs I suppose. The only difference was that she found me attractive also.

'I love you too,' I said awkwardly. I had never said those words to anyone before and would never tell another woman again. I wish I could have stayed there with Marie forever, watching the ocean and sun rise and fall. But alas, I had promises to keep and work to do. Such was the life of a smuggler.

CHAPTER 13

I had not had much time to rest from my adventures in France. We had a cargo to distribute, and it had been hauled into Prussia Cove by some lads who I had poached from the local farms. Bessie would purchase what she wanted first, but that left a considerable amount out in the open. The caves at the cove could hold a large amount of goods. Yet it wasn't deep enough for my liking and I wanted to excavate it, to make it even larger. It would need to be too, if we were to bring in the amount of goods I hoped we would from France.

We worked a sweat up, loading the many barrels onto shore.

When my ship was just about emptied, a rider dismounted at the top of the cliffs, and waved his hands down to us urgently, shouting something I could not quite hear. I ran up to meet him to see what all the fuss was.

'John, I've come to warn you, the duty men are coming; a bloody lot of them too!' I turned back quickly and looked at my landed cargo with horror. If a riding officer caught me with it, I would lose my fortune once more, and be lucky to avoid the gallows.

The King of Prussia Cove

'How much time do we have man!' I said to him hurriedly, thinking fast for solutions on how to hide the tubs of spirit. I never liked the way some smuggler dropped them into the sea with stones. Only to come back later, diluted with enough sea water to sour the taste for even the hardiest of drinkers. I would need to find another way to keep my cargo and its quality.

'About an hour away, maybe two. I heard them in town getting excited to come here. I left as they were saddling their horses. I reckon they'll be slow getting here,' he informed me helpfully. I threw him some coins, which he pocketed in seconds, and looked past him noticing his powerful looking horse munching the lush grass happily. An idea was beginning to form in my head. It would be a close shave, but if I acted with haste, I could get away with the cargo and my life.

'If you help me with my goods, I'll double that coin?' I said pleadingly. He agreed, and I told him my plan, while running back to the lads to set them to the task. They were used to this sort of thing happening and, snapped to it eagerly.

I remembered that just down the bridle path which wound east of where we were, was an old mine shaft that had been abandoned long ago. To lug all the cargo there would take a monumental effort, so I sent lads to recruit folk who were in Bessie's beer house to my cause. James and William both frantically pulled tub after tub up the hill and we managed to hire some more horses that had been tied outside of Bessie's place. Even Marie helped in the chain of men, aiding our deliverance.

We managed to squirrel the lot away in an unbelievably fast time. It took about an hour and a quarter to roll in the last tub, and then head back to the cove absolutely numb with fatigue. The riding officers came very shortly after, trailed by a small contingent of dragoons. We were sitting on the cliff top; trying to appear like we were relaxing in the afternoon sun, but the dripping sweat and puffed faces contradicted our leisurely deception.

The rider at the head of the group was none other than Arthur The Ferret Ferris, who I'd heard had built quite a reputation as a ruthless customs rider. He was hated by the local community who now shunned him at every turn. It would never bother him whether he was liked though. He had crossed that line long ago, and was content with the bed he lay in.

I saw his pock ridden face under his hat, looking triumphant at seeing the smugglers out in broad daylight, and easy pickings for him and his men. As he noticed me I stood, towering over the rest of the lads who I was with.

The colour of his skin turned several shades paler. He looked like he had seen a ghost. That was understandable; for all he knew, I was dead or rotting inside a French prison.

Later I heard that he found out about my ship full of goods by his usual tricks of overhearing conversations. No one had been foolish enough to mention my name, and by the shock on his face when he saw me, that was obvious.

'Hello Arthur. Say; you look like you're having a funny turn. Are you feeling alright?' I said, trying to hide the fact that I was still out of breath from hiding the cargo. He remained mounted, and regained some of his composure, bringing his horse close to me. He menacingly circled my group, attempting to intimidate us. Then stopped and pulled a pistol from a holster at the side of his mount, pointing it straight at me.

His men had obviously expected a fight from us, and they in turn drew weapons of all descriptions.

We just sat there, trying to appear as relaxed as possible. 'You're finished Carter! You should have stayed away. It's just as well for me you didn't. Search the cove and beer house Mr Davis!' he shouted over to another customs rider, who dismounted and led some men all around the cove and into Bessie's place. He would not find anything, and after about thirty minutes they returned to tell The Ferret of their lack of success. 'Keep looking you fools, it's here somewhere,' he ordered his men red faced.

'You won't find anything sir. We have no cargo. I have been in Guernsey for a while, and I've returned to do a bit of fishing here. No law against that is there?' I said to him knowing full well that he knew I had not come for the fish.

The King of Prussia Cove

He drew a light cavalry sword from his horse and dismounted, handing the rains to one of his men. He had the power here, and since I thought he would never find the contraband, I didn't fight him from fear of the consequences, for both me and my men. It was a hanging offence to attack a customs man. He would have loved it if I had tried. So instead, I stood my ground and waited.

With the heavy pommel of his sword he hit me on the cheek with a mighty crack. The noise of the strike betrayed the cheekbone he had fractured, and I fell to the floor in a heap. My men moved to draw knives, but I had sense enough to shout a warning to halt their actions in time. 'Do nothing! They have nothing, and we have nothing to fear,' I said to the men as I nursed my face, which had already begun to swell.

'You disappoint me Carter; I thought you liked a good fight. Not that your father did of course. But he can't do anything now he's six feet under, can he?'

I could have killed him for that. I had to control myself; a feat that had proved difficult at the mention of my father. He wanted me to attack him. It took all my will power to remain calm, but calm I was in the face of the man I hated so much.

'Just do what you came here for and be damned Arthur,' I replied with visible fury. He looked out to where my small cutter was anchored and looked pleased when another sloop sailed into the cove and made its way alongside mine.

'Ah… there they are. You better not have anything you shouldn't have on that vessel Carter. I think we will confiscate her as well. You can't anchor this close to shore for more than an hour. It's the rules I'm afraid,' he said to me triumphantly. 'Come on lads, let's go. Mr Davis, stay here and secure theses wretches. You Carter can come with me. It's your ship after all,' he indicated. Either way he would not be leaving empty handed. I knew the rules just as any smuggler did. He was correct in saying that the ship was his if he could prove we had been there for over an hour. He had kept us secured for a good while, and I would argue that case later at the magistrates. For the time being though, I just kept quiet and let him row me out with a small contingent of his customs officers.

I had some men on board washing down the decks when they were taken by surprise by the customs sloop. I heard a pistol fire and I hoped and prayed that none of my men had been killed mistaking the customs sloop as pirates.

We climbed aboard and the lads I had left were all in irons, with one bleeding heavily from his hand. It was Daniel Smith, and he was shrieking in agony at the loss of one of his fingers. 'What's going on? We're just a fishing vessel!' I shouted at the customs officer who had taken over my ship. His pistol smoked from the shot he had taken at my man, and he drew a rapier and advanced on me, coming within inches of its wicked point. The man holding the sword was the same man who had tried to have me arrested before, for claiming the floating booty just off Penzance.

George Scrobel looked murderous with that weapon. He had probably expected trouble from us too when he boarded and was taking no chances.

I instinctively backed away, nearly knocking The Ferret over the guard rail and into the blue waters below. He stopped the point level with my swollen eye, and almost looked disappointed that we hadn't tried to resist them.

'Did you find anything on land Arthur?' he asked The Ferret irritably.

'Nothing; but the men are still searching. It won't be long before we do,' he replied to his fellow duty man.

'Turn this ship inside out. If he's got even a drop of what he shouldn't, I want to know about it.' he ordered his men, who began their search in earnest.

'You will find nothing; you're wasting your time sir,' I tried to say with confidence I did not feel. I knew the lads had emptied the ship, but there was always a chance that someone had slipped up and forgotten something. I prayed once again and felt that God had perhaps been toying with me for my sins. I had after all just been released from captivity with the French, only managing to keep my possessions with bargaining. With these men on the other hand, no bargain could be made. They only sought my ruin and would employ any means to do so.

When one of the duty men appeared from the cargo hold, I realised just how low they would stoop to catch an honest smuggler such as I.

'I've found this sir!' said the customs man excitedly, holding a package in his hand. He brought it to his commander and opened the oiled skin to reveal dark and damming tobacco.

I knew with upmost certainty that it was not mine. The swine had framed me well and proper, and I was forced to think fast for our very lives.

Blood had pooled on the deck from Daniel's wound. His agonising screams had been haunting for all to hear. Unhelpfully the seagulls matched poor Daniel scream for scream and dove down to the deck plucking up his severed finger, which laid too temptingly for them to resist.

'Hey… that's my bloody finger,' he shouted at them as they jumped up and away with their prize. The customs men all laughed at his misfortune, and I could hold my tongue no longer.

'You sir have attacked an unarmed man going about his business. I will seek reparation for the injury caused. Make no mistake about that.' My anger was at boiling point, and I swatted the sword point away from my face with as much contempt as I could muster. Scrobel must have thought I was attacking him and came back at me prodding his blade, aiming for my heart. I turned at the last minute, taking the wicked point in left shoulder.

Now I was the one crying out in pain, and instinctively, I grabbed hold of the rapier with my hand, and should have let go when he pulled the blade back. It sliced my hand open, but the cut was so clean I could not even feel the wound.

After a pause my own blood began to pour from the gash he had sliced.

Before I could launch any kind of defence, I felt the cold steel of another blade touch my neck gently. It was as tender as a kiss, and I stopped immediately, thinking my life was about to be taken. I put my hands up in surrender, slowly, without causing alarm.

'I would like nothing more than to cut your throat Carter. But I would rather see you hang; and hang you will for attacking a customs official. What a pity,' Arthur Ferris said, as he held his own sword on me steadily. He added just enough pressure so as not to break the skin.

'You know that's not mine,' I said, gritting my teeth from my injuries. 'That's all irrelevant now Carter; your men on shore might escape the noose. You and these lads here though, will dance a merry jig for your actions.'

I had never seen him look so happy. One of his men had noticed one of my sloops sailing off east and shouted a warning to Scrobel.

'There's some getting away sir!'

'Don't worry; we have what we came for. Secure this vessel. We're going,' Scrobel announced finally.

I was given a piece of rag to wrap my hand in, and they were kind enough to tie some padding to my wounded shoulder, which bleed less than my hand but no less painful.

Daniel's dripping stump, where his finger had once been, was also wrapped up in rag, and had needed changing every five minutes due to its claret saturation.

Wounded and broken, my spirits dropped at the cruel twist of fate. I was about to earn a fortune with my new French partner. But once again my liberty had been taken from me, with another trap concocted by the treacherous Ferret.

I took small comfort when the sloop sailed east towards Penzance. I had expected to be taken there if I was arrested.

When we were warned about the arrival of the customs men, I had told William and James to hide a sloop we owned out of sight. When the customs sloop anchored they were to make a dash to pay a visit to the home of my friend Arthur, who I suspected would be in attendance with the other customs men.

I knew they would find a way to take us for something, and put us under arrest, even without the French spirits.

So, I sent them off into the early evening to enter The Ferret's house and acquire an insurance policy if things took a turn for the worst. After all; he did not know that we knew he was an agent of France. I hoped that we would gain a priceless bargaining piece on which to fight our accusers. But I would have to wait to see if my desperate plan had worked.

CHAPTER 14

The trial was set for two weeks' time, and I must say that our wait was far less comfortable than France. It was a daily challenge to keep the rats away from nibbling at us incessantly.

By the time we were presented in court, I was in a really sorry state indeed.

To my pleasant surprise, John Tonkin had arranged for us to have legal representation by a man who would become as valuable to me as any gold or diamonds. His name was Christopher Wallis, an attorney to many a smuggler, and a man who I could trust with my life.

I had been mightily impressed upon first meeting him. He wore an expensive wig, and his shirt and coat were of the finest quality. He was not a particularly tall man, and I towered over him when I was questioned at length about what had occurred. His lack of height was irrelevant when he spoke to me. He was enigmatic, passionate, and had a powerful voice that would have been the envy of any preacher or politician. He was an orator of legend, and folk would become entranced when he presented an argument.

The King of Prussia Cove

Christopher Wallis knew what we were and told us that Mr Tonkin was making arrangements to have the spirits we hid, had been moved to a safer location.

I told him what had happened to us on board my ship, and how they had planted the small pouch of tobacco. He told me that he could argue away the packet of tobacco, but the assault upon the customs men would prove a difficult task, even for someone with his legal prowess. I told him all about The Ferret, and how we may have gained a trump card for our trial.

'Your friends came to me this morning and told me the same,' he said to me enthusiastically. 'They have brought me something very damning indeed regarding Mr Ferris. But we should only use it if we must. Let events play out a tad eh,' he added.

A small group of us sat in the dock awaiting the Magistrate Walter Borlace. The jury were already seated, and I winked and nodded in greeting to the many them I knew well. I had sold duty free contraband to folk from here to Falmouth and knew a great deal of my clients who I had dealt with honestly. I expected to be treated in kind for the good relationships I had built with the townsfolk present among the Jury.

I could see Robert Hatton the local Butcher, and William Trim, a bricklayer who I had also done some business with. The only problem was our judge Mr Borlace, who would press us greatly. They had been very active catching smugglers, and he was an advocate for our end.

He entered the courtroom and sat himself before us on his lofty perch. The customs officer George Scrobel sat alongside Arthur Ferris, who now stood and told the court his account of events.

'I was informed your honour, that a smuggling vessel was unloading goods without paying the duty owed to the king. I then raced there with all speed and found that most of the goods had been taken away or hidden. We did however find a small amount of tobacco which the defendants failed to conceal from us. That's when they attempted to cause us harm and avoid the justice of the law sir. We had to defend ourselves in the process, and eventually apprehended them all.' The Ferrets account failed to mention that they attacked us first, and the tobacco found was planted by them. There was no way to prove this of course; so, our attorney went down a different tact in our defence.

'Your honour, the gentlemen before you, are only guilty of plucking a parcel of tobacco from the sea. They were then set upon by the duty men, offering no provocation what's so ever. Mr Carter here has been struck on the face, stabbed, and had his hand cut open. He swears, as do his men, that they were willing to co-operate with the authorities, who behaved more like pirates than lawmen. They even shot off the finger of another innocent man who is here today. I hope the members of the jury can see reason and find the men here not guilty. The poor souls were only trying to catch fish when this misfortune swept them away,' Christopher Wallis said with much emotion. We had the sympathies of the jurors already. But after his opening statement I knew we had them on the most part.

A few that clearly did not favour us shook their heads and rolled their eyes. We would have to win them over if we were to avoid punishment.

We had informers feeding back to us how the jury were split. It did not look promising, even with our amazing defence. It was time to play our top card.

After two days, the trial was nearing its end and would soon conclude for good or ill. William Vingoe sat down the evening before the third day at the table of Arthur Ferris and told him what we knew.

'Are you missing some letters Mr Ferris?' he had said to him.

'I don't know what you're talking about,' The Ferret replied; clearly flustered, but not giving away much.

'Well, we have some very traitorous letters written to you sir. And we have witnesses who will swear that you regularly meet with French speaking gentlemen.'

'What do you want?' he said angrily and reached down to his pistol. He knew the letters were missing. He also knew they were addressed to him. William told me how satisfying it was to see the terror on his face.

'There is no need for that sir,' William said, calming The Ferret's hand. 'All we require of you is to make this unsavoury situation go away. You must say in court tomorrow that you may have been a tad too eager in your attempt to apprehend the lads in the dock. And that they may have mistaken you for pirates after all.' William produced one of the letters to show the truth of his claim.

'We have more where this came from sir. I hope you choose wisely,' William claimed finally and left The Ferret steaming in fury.

I laughed at the story, and as expected Arthur stood and gave his final account to a confused looking Walter Borlace and jury.

'Are you sure that is what happened sir?' said the bewildered magistrate, who would have quite happily have sent us all to our deaths that morning.

'Yes sir. I may have been a bit over zealous in my actions. They could have very well confused us as bandits on reflection your honour,' The Ferret said with his head down.

'Very well sir, I will take that into account,' the Magistrate concluded.

We adjourned to let the jury conclude, which they did promptly. On the count of assaulting the customs officers we were found unsurprisingly, not guilty, and my friends in the court gave a small cheer and clapped. The Magistrate's hammer fell with annoyance to silence our celebrations.

There was still the matter of the tobacco to decide upon.

To my dismay, I was found guilty for smuggling the small amount of contraband which was hard to argue over. The tobacco was always going to cause trouble for us, but at least we had a chance not to hang for it.

Although it was not unheard of for an ill-tempered magistrate to don the black cap for petty offences such as we had committed.

I volunteered myself as acting alone in this, thus saving my friends and crew from any punishment.

The sentence was for me alone. I said I had pulled the goods on board to sell for my own ends. The lads appreciated my gesture, and it would be remembered for years to come.

The magistrate gave me a choice of two years hard labour or service in the navy. The choice was a simple one.

I was allowed a moment to decide, and while contemplating the next two years my friend William Vingoe came to me, as I sat trying figure how I could wriggle out of yet another mess I had gotten into.

'You know that you can nominate someone else to join the navy if your purse is heavy enough John,' he said to me helpfully. I knew that to be true. If I decided to take the service in the navy, I could pay someone to go in my stead. A strange rule, but one I could utilise if only I had the funds. Alas, until I sold the cargo, I had nothing. I told William this and he nodded sympathetically.

'You know what my friend. I never did thank you properly for coming to our aid against those Irish pirates,' he told me. In truth he had given me my freedom to do what I loved in the world of smuggling. In my eyes he owed me no thanks.

'To be honest with you John, I would quite like to join the admiralty any way. It can be quite lucrative I hear. Let me do this for you, and we will be even eh.'

'You owe me nothing William. It is I that holds gratitude to you. I have never had a better friend and partner.'

'That is kind of you to say. But I want to go. Let me do this for you,' he said with utter sincerity. In the end I relented and agreed. At the time I had felt tremendous guilt at sending my dear friend into the hands of the admiralty. But this unique opportunity would make my friend William Vingoe a legend in his own right, and a very rich man.

With the arrangement made, I was now free once more. William left with a merry heart and told us he looked forward to commandeering us if we crossed paths jokingly.

I was now acutely aware that I had a target on my back, which the customs men would love to take aim at. They would surly try to hit their mark.

CHAPTER 15

The war in Europe was heating up. Prussia was surrounded on all sides, with Sweden allying themselves with the French, Russians and Austrians against them. Over the war years, King Fredrick would overcome insurmountable odds to win a kind of stalemate. On the succession of Tsar Peter III in 1762, Russia changed sides, and Prussia had emerged from the conflict as a new super power of Europe.

Britain were also faring well and were gaining territories in French America east of the Mississippi river, parts of Canada, and several Caribbean islands.

My friend William Vingoe had earned himself a place on a cutter named the Wolf, where he had been quickly promoted to first officer and Lieutenant, for his uncanny navel abilities.

I could have kept my head down and lived a peaceful life, fishing and topping up my income from smuggling here and there. But my ambitions had no limits, and after the trial I resumed my activities straight away.

The first task was to distribute what I'd already acquired. Most of it was sitting in the same mine shaft where we had hidden it. The rest, James had sold locally.

Once I was back controlling things, it took no time at all to get rid of the rest of it. I had assumed the customs men would have been too embarrassed to continue their harassment after their last efforts. I was wrong unfortunately.

Every town and village I entered, the dreaded duty men plagued our movements, making our jobs difficult to say the least. Not impossible; just difficult.

I decided to make arrangements to strengthen our hand. I could not let myself or my cargo be taken again, so soon after the last calamities. I asked Samuel The Poacher to join our merry band. He would be the perfect protection for us if things became violent. Samuels aim with any weapon was legendary. Just the sight of him would make any aggressor think twice.

The power of the musket and rifle was undisputed.

Samuel preferred the rifle for its accuracy and lethality, as musket shot over any reasonable distance became luck more than skill. But the rifle which he carried, would make the round spin in mid-flight, and kept the round on its intending path. It was slower to load, but its accuracy was worth that small concession.

If events turned into a fire fight and multiple rounds were required to fight off an enemy, Samuel would have a weapon for that scenario as well. He was never without his powerful longbow, and a quiver full of sharply pointed arrows. I asked him why he carried such a primitive weapon, when he could just have a pistol and rifle.

'The rifle is good John; very good actually. But in the thick of a fight, I can let fly three arrow shafts before the first one has hit its mark. No one can stand under that rate of fire power. It's how we beat the French at Agincourt. They had cross bows that were accurate and could be shot by a mere novice. The longbow on the other hand needed to be used by someone t who'd trained with them for most of their lives. The strength required is considerable I might add. But if mastered, no musket, rifle or anything in existence can compete with the old longbow,' he said to me as a matter of fact.

I asked him to teach me how to shoot a pistol and rifle, to which he kindly instructed.

I was a good fighter, but my expertise with weapons was not the best, and I intended to change that fact. When I had first met William Vingoe and watched him wield his blade so masterfully, I also beseeched him to teach me the arts of the sword. I was more of a brawler with the weapon at first and used its edge more like a club than a weapon of beauty. But I am a fast learner. It did not take me long to give William a run for his money, in our many mock duels. After a while I had become very competent indeed with most blades.

Samuel was like my tutor for projectile weaponry. We practiced on the cliff tops, shooting targets that we had made up from old barrels, and bales of hay. I would never have an eye for targets like he had. But once again I learned his teachings fast. After about six months I became a crack shot with rifle, pistol and bow. I loved practicing so much that I had to stop myself sometimes and remember that business needed my attention, which was more important than playing with weapons. It had indeed felt like play. It was almost as if we were small children again, with our sticks and stones to fight our mock battles with.

My ship was making run after run to our agreed meeting point with Lieutenant Domenici. For the first voyages over to the Continent, I was in attendance to ensure the trade was carried out smoothly, and without misshape. But after several successful cargos had been landed, I decided to stay on land and do what I was good at, which was distribution. The caves were filling up and we couldn't get rid of the ever-incoming cargoes from France fast enough. This was a good thing of course, because the goods we were buying were in such high demand. My only problem was storage on our side at Prussia Cove.

A warehouse would have been the ideal thing. But we couldn't very well build such storage, which would act like a beacon for any customs rider to poke around. There were two alternatives I could take. Move my base of business or extend and excavate the caves at Prussia Cove. The choice once again was simple. A king does not abandon his kingdom after all.

After years of trying to escape the mines and digging, I was back underground with pick and hammer to carve our secret contraband store. Locally, there was many a miner out of work, and I approached a few of my old friends who I could trust. I tried to be as involved as I could but left most of the tunnelling to my younger brother Charles, who had come to work at the cove full time. He cheerfully kept the project going and was a perfect choice to oversee its progress, due to his talent as a miner, and his agreeable nature that everyone loved about him.

My romance with Marie continued, and one rainy day, I came into Bessie's place for some stew and ale, when she took me to one side. 'John, I have something to tell you.'

'What is it? You're not going to propose to me are you Marie?' I said jokingly. The prospect of marriage had been on my mind, but I was too busy trying to make a name for myself to have the time to settle down. I smiled and when I realised that she did not share my humour, I took her hands and asked. 'Come on, what is it?'

A lonely tear crept slowly down her exquisite cheek, and I wiped it away with the cuff of my shirt. She looked at me with trepidation, and I thought in that moment she would say that she did not love me any longer. She took a few deep breaths and her bosoms rose and fell like the swell of the ocean.

'I am with child John,' she cried finally, and could not bear to look at my wide-eyed shock. I was young but should have known better. But I was still surprised I'd be a father.

Shock, quickly turned to wonder and euphoria. I was going to be a father. I picked her up and spun her easily around, whooping in delight. 'What's got you two so excited?' Bessie her mother called over.

I didn't take my eyes from my love, as I answered old Bess.

'I just asked your daughter to marry me Bess, if that's alright by you?' Marie's tears stopped, as did the rain outside the beer house.

A ray of light shone in through the murky windows, illuminating our moods further.

'You will marry me won't you my love?' I asked quietly, so only she could hear me. 'You're not cross with me?' she replied blushing. I shook my head. How could I ever be cross with her?

'Never... this is the best of news. So, will you? Will you be my Mrs Carter, and my Queen of Prussia Cove?' I asked expectantly. To my relief, she did not hesitate.

'I will John, I will,' she confirmed, and leaned in to kiss me passionately.

We didn't care that her mother was standing right behind us, or the other lads, who all grinned at our small romantic display.

For us in that moment, no other soul on Gods Earth existed.

We celebrated long into the night and when the place emptied out; Bessie came over to me and filled my cup with gin.

Marie had long since turned in for the night, which left me alone with her mother. She knew we were fond on each other, and never scolded us for our frolicking behaviour. Her temper was well known however, and she could throw out the unruliest of customers, with the help of the many sharp knives and clubs which she kept under the bar. I had seen her use them to devastating effect, and I hoped she was not about to stick one of them in me for deflowering her dear daughter.

'This used to be such a quiet place before you came along John Carter.'

'I am sorry Bess,' I replied nervously.

'Don't be sorry lad. Business has never been so good, and I was bored to tell you the truth.' She looked pensively at a rough portrait of her dead husband. He was also a successful smuggler and fisherman, and I would often catch her staring at his image when she had drunk too much grog.

'He would've been happy that his daughter has met a man like you. I am happy. But promise me something?' she asked me emotionally.

'I will,' I agreed.

'Don't get killed too young. You have ambition just like my poor husband had. A lot of good it did him when the customs men shot holes in him. I don't wish the same fate for my Marie.'

I understood completely. She feared her one and only child would become a widow like her, and spend the days pinning for her lost love.

'I am a miner's son Bess, and his father before him slaved down a shaft, until a painful and early death claimed them. I stand before you now a wealthy man. My children will never see the inside of a blasted mine. I will make you this promise though. I will not throw my life away like, so many smugglers do. I will become the best at what I do, and your daughter will never go hungry, nor want for anything again. If we are blessed to have a child, then they shall also want for nothing. Will you accept that promise?' I said with pride and conviction.

Bess nodded at me and smiled kindly. She rarely did that. If she liked you, then she would often jab you with a dinner fork or argue for no reason at all. If she did not like you, then you were simply ignored, and sometimes expelled from her beer house without warning. When she had sat down at my table, I had expected to be ejected like a mangy dog. Instead she had welcomed me into her family. Her side of the cove, known as Bessie's Cove would now formally unite in alliance with my Prussia Cove. My small realm was expanding it seemed.

CHAPTER 16

We set a wedding date for one month's time. It was the beginning of a blistering summer, and I remember how stifling the church was, with so many well-wishers crammed in to see us tie the knot. I was the eldest of my nine brothers and sisters, who all stood in the front two pews. My brother Charles stood as my best man, and the ceremony was carried out by none other than John Wesley, who had been spreading the Methodist movement and the word of God in the sinful county of Cornwall with great success.

He was aware what I did to make a living. Most people did by then, and I made it my purpose in life to make them aware of it. The Customs men knew it too, but what could they do if they couldn't prove any wrong doing.

I was scalded before the ceremony began, as John Wesley pulled me to one side.

'Smuggling is a sinful affair Mr Carter; you should cease your activities in that line of work, especially now you are going to be married,' he said to me outside the church sternly.

The King of Prussia Cove

I knew him well. I always tried to hear him preach when I could. He was a wise and godly man and brought the spirit closer to the Lord in ways that other preachers could not come close to. On the issue of smuggling however, I had to disagree with him.

'I realise there are much nobler professions I could occupy myself with. But I cannot agree that free trade is a sin. The rich are at it, and the government, nay the Lord himself turns a blind eye. When a man of lower birth does well for himself, then he is a criminal. I am an honest man sir, and I fear the wrath of God for my other sins. I just can't count feeding myself, and my family as one of them,' I replied to him with as much reason that I could muster. I did not want to anger the man who was just about to marry me.

'Your arguments are compelling Mr Carter. I still hold on to my principles, but I must say, if you do continue with smuggling, do it with the Lord in your heart,' he suggested as a way of compromise. 'I will,' I said.

Moments later I was about to say, I will again, in a promise to love and care for my wife to be Marie. I had given her money to purchase the finest garments from a dress maker in Helston. She wore an equally fine wig, but I insisted she wear little makeup or powder on her face. She was far too beautiful to cover herself up with a mask of paleness. I never liked the fashion of patting the face with powder for the sake of beauty, and a beauty she was.

She could have held my gaze forever.

I cannot remember the words I said to her that day. I was too entranced and thrilled at the same time, that I would be marrying Marie; my love.

I do remember the party we held afterwards though, and we danced and sang late into the night. We ate pork off the bone, beef pies and washed it down with a very considerable amount of French claret. A perk of my profession I suppose.

John Tonkin provided us with a fine wedding cake that we shared out to our grateful guests, who all told me that they could not remember a merrier wedding.

It was also my intention to mix a bit of business with pleasure. Weddings I would learn were an excellent time to do deals with people. The reason behind this idea was that there would be a large group of folks all together at the same time, so I would not have to travel to them to ask what I could in one evening.

They were also plied with wine, spirits and ale. Fine weapons indeed to lubricate price negotiations; and because I had supplied the food and drink, most were gratefully generous when we eventually struck a bargain.

I wanted to speak to one man in particular that night, and as Marie sat with my mother and her own, gossiping about who knew what. I was making the deal of a lifetime with a man named Richard Richardson.

He was a wool merchant who didn't live far from Marazion.

I had done countless deals with Richard and thanked him for accepting my invitation. 'I'm happy to come to such a wonderful event John. Congratulations to you and your lovely wife,' he said, chewing on a piece of straw contently.

'I wanted to come and talk to you sooner, but I've been occupied as you can imagine.' I was, trying to lead the conversation to business. I had mentioned to him before that I might be in the market to purchase extremely large quantities of wool from him. Now that I had him merry from copious amounts of grog I had sent his way, I asked if we could do a deal.

'I want to buy as much wool as you can get your hands-on Richard, but the movement of goods needs to be kept quite if you catch my meaning.'

'Are you going into the wool business now John? I thought you were a man of the sea from what I hear, quite a successful one too.'

'I still am, and that will be my means of transport. I can't say who my buyer is, for your own good. But I was wondering Richard, if you will give me time to pay you for it. I can guarantee payment, and you know I am good for it after our many dealings' I paused and waited for him to digest what I had asked.

The price of wool on the continent was high. English wool was well known to be of the best quality anywhere. The same could be said about French brandy, and claret, which was becoming hard for an Englishman to get his hands on.

I was however bringing in the stuff by the ton load.

Incidentally, Lieutenant Domenici could make a considerable amount of money if he could get his hand on Cornish wool. In truth, I had the money to buy the wool outright. But credit was even better, and I stated an offer of what I would pay him per ton for any wool he could supply me with.

His eyes lit up greedily, just as I knew they would. Richard Richardson had been buying smuggled goods from me for a long time now, and I was confident he would accept the risk to fatten his purse. It was not unusual to ask a merchant for credit, but he also had to allow for the risk of the cargo being taken by the duty men, for wool had an exorbitant export tax upon it. If they found out I was selling to the French, I would also be once again in serious trouble. The concerned look on Richard's face told me he had the same concerns.

'Don't fret about the customs men Richard. I'm good at what I do, and if things go sour, I would die before I gave them your name,' I said trying to persuade him. He nodded slowly and started to stroke his chin. I had noticed him doing that the last time we had negotiated for a sale of gin.

I decided I would add an extra word to sooth his concerns. 'If you like Richard, we could do a small deal and see how it goes. Plus, I will give you ten percent extra to make it even more lucrative your end.' He nodded some more, still stroking his chin for comfort.

'If the first deal goes well John; let's say I let you buy two tons. How much wool will you trade after that?' he asked, clearly leaning towards taking the deal. 'I can buy and sell as much as you can supply. My buyers demand is that high, we will be extremely rich men if the wool flows in large quantities. I can handle the transport from your markets to my ships. Then you'll only have to wait a month or two until payment is given. I can assure you that the smuggled wool will not be associated to you in any way. Just leave it in a pre-arranged spot, and I will send my lads to collect.'

We shook on the deal there and then, and we both parted feeling happy with ourselves.

I was pleased to have married Marie that day. But the wool I had negotiated to buy from Richard Richardson, put me one step closer to becoming the man of means I always aspired to be.

I took the liberty to make other deals that day too.

I sold gin, brandy, pepper, and tea, among many other items that I could acquire though my usual channels. All I would have to do was organise the delivery of goods and collect payment.

Most folk had heard about my scuffles and martial prowess, and all paid on time without quarrel because of that fact.

However, if there ever was trouble, I could always send Samuel The Poacher to collect a debt. He was even more reputable than I was. It took a brave person to refuse the burly crack shot.

He normally had a blunderbuss with him for difficult customers. It was not a weapon of beauty and fired many small shot. At close range the blast from a blunderbuss could be devastating and could quite easily tear a limb clean from a body. But thankfully no one ever negated on a promised deal when I sent old Samuel to remind them of their obligation.

After the wedding, Marie and I took up residence in Bessie's beer house, to the joy of her mother who enjoyed my company.

I liked living close to my Prussia Cove too, where all our business was being launched from. With a wee babe on the way, I didn't want to stay cooped up in the small rooms above the beer house for any longer than I had to.

With that in mind, I paid a visit to Lord Arundell's Steward, John Treluddra, and asked for the opportunity to purchase land.

I had expected to make my fortune that year, and I informed Mr Treluddra of my dealings, to which he and Lord Arundell would receive their share of the profits.

I could have operated without paying them a penny of course. But men of influence were always good to have on your side.

My consistent contribution to Lord Arundell had put me in good stead with him and his wife the Lady Arundell, who always asked about my adventures. From then until this day, the Arundell's have always looked out for me and my kin.

I wanted to purchase the land around Prussia Cove, which included Pixy Cove and Bessie's Cove. I asked to buy a few acres inland as well, because I wanted to look to the future and extend my small kingdom as much as I could. I also asked to purchase the farm where my mother still dwelt with my younger brothers and sisters.

Mr Treluddra returned a week later and agreed to my offer with two conditions. The first was that any spoils from the wrecking of ships around the coves, was to go to Lord Arundell. The second condition was that I go and see his lordship personally. He would very rarely mix with lower born men such as me, so I was honoured to go, and agreed to both conditions readily.

CHAPTER 17

I had purchased a fine stallion from a horse dealer who sold the best animals to the British Cavalry. I called the horse Francis after my father.

He was stubborn like him, and powerfully built to travel across the craggy Cornish countryside. I also purchased a fine saddle and concealed my many weapons within the pockets which I had asked to be added to the leatherwork. I also used the secret pockets to hide large amounts of money I would often carry with me.

On my way to see Lord Arundell, it was practically bursting with coin to buy my land. I was making so much money from my deals in Franc after all. I hoped if he agreed to sell me the land, I would not need a mortgage to acquire what I wanted.

I dismounted and led old Francis down the gravel path to the Arundell's house. Two dogs came running towards me, both barking, but were so small I didn't feel threatened. As they neared I noticed that they had been dressed in dog sized human outfits, and even had small wigs clipped to their heads. They looked better attired than I did, and I was wearing my finest cloths.

I thought how incredible it was that a person would dress their animals up as humans. But the rich people, I would learn quickly, ran out of ways to spend their money and amuse themselves. Some of their pets lived a better existence than most working men.

I would never waste good coin on trivialities like that, and I am no worse for it. But everyone to their own I suppose.

I shooed the two terriers away, and I was greeted by Mr Treluddra who led me to their library. I had never seen so many books in all my life, until I witnessed the Arundell collection, which spanned from floor to ceiling high above. There was a mahogany ladder on wheels providing access to the books on the loftier shelves.

I could read well enough and looking at the uncountable volumes stacked neatly in their leather-bound casings, I could very well have stayed in that room for a hundred years and still not have exhausted the near limitless supply of books.

I noticed such authors as Voltaire, William Whitehead and Henry Brookes Collection of Fairy Tales.

Spending time on ships gave a man plenty of time to read if he was inclined to do so. I would read whenever I could and made a note to purchase a few of the popular novels on display in the library.

'Impressive, is it not Mr Carter?' a voice said behind me, taking my attention away from the books. 'It is very impressive my Lord. I haven't seen anything like it in all my days.'

Lord Arundell, joined me with two brandies in his hands. He offered me one and I accepted, taking a sip of the smooth liquor to settle my nerves.

It slid down my throat and I welcomed the numbing relief it gave me.

'Do you read lad?' he asked me curiously. I did not take offence from his question. Many working men did not read, and the ones that could did not read well.

'I do sir. John Wesley himself taught me to read. I must confess that I'm envious of your collection.'

'Wesley, eh... The Methodist?' he inquired with interest.

'Yes. He encouraged us to read well, so we may better understand the word of the Lord,' I replied.

Lord Arundell pulled a book and opened its pages, squinting slightly to read the words within.

'Do you like Voltaire Mr Carter? He is one of my favourite writers, even though he is French… Here' He handed me the book and I examined the cover. 'It's called Zandig or The Book of Fate. The story is about a philosopher from Babylonia. A fascinating read I might add.'

'I will be sure to purchase a copy my Lord.'

'You may take this one if you wish, I have other copies. It's written in French though, a tongue I understand you have become quite acquainted in,' he subtly mentioned, to let me know that he knew about my activities in France. I had suspected he had known, being a patron to John Tonkin, who was also involved in my French dealings. I decided to answer him vaguely.

'That is very kind of you sir, I do speak French well enough I suppose. It sounds like an interesting story.'

'Stories of destiny always are. Your story one day would make a good book I would warrant. My wife has been begging to hear about your smuggling adventures… Marvellous for a man so young. I wanted to talk to you first though. My wife can pester you later?'

I placed the book in a leather satchel I had slung over my shoulder and waited for him to talk.

'Mr Treluddra has told me that you wish to purchase some land from me. I have thought it through, and your offer is very generous for the acres you desire,' he said reasonably.

I had offered over the value for the land, not wanting to insult him with bargaining. This was one man after all that could bring a sudden halt to my activities. I stayed silent and let him continue.

'Very generous indeed; I must say Mr Carter that you have already placed great wealth into my hands over these past years, and I want to show you my appreciation.'

We had never discussed the money I had been sending him for allowing me and my lads to smuggle goods on his land. It had been

The King of Prussia Cove

a silent partnership until now, with John Tonkin taking care of the Lord's desires, regarding what I was up to. I had always paid well, hoping that if an occasion like this came up, he would treat me favourably.

'You are most welcome sir, I am grateful for all the help you have given me,' I said sincerely. He had no doubt financed most of my larger cargo purchases, even if it had come through John Tonkin.

'I want to offer you the land you have asked for. I will accept half of what you have offered for it,' he offered generously. I tried not to stand opened mouthed and look as simple as I felt.

'That is very good my Lord. Is there anything I could do for you in way of thanks?'

John Treluddra had hinted that Lord Arundell may ask a favour of me, and I was making it as easy as possible for him to ask. I could have been signing my own death warrant for all I knew, but I would always help the people that helped me in return. That is the way of commerce and prosperity. When one hand washes the other as such.

'I would like to be candid if I may,' he said.

'Of course,' I replied.

'I have interests and a cargo to be transported from Jamaica, and because of the war with France, I am struggling to find ships to collect this cargo. I was wondering if you would be willing to go to Jamaica on my behalf.' He looked at me hopefully, and I must say that I was not entirely sure I wanted to leave my country for so long, on a voyage as treacherous as we both knew it was.

'What's the cargo my Lord, and why me?' I asked, hoping to buy time and think more on what he was asking me to do for him. He could have asked many merchant captains to collect his cargo for him. I wanted to know why he had asked me.

'The cargo is sugar. It has already been refined and is awaiting transportation as we speak on behalf of William Beckford who is a member of parliament and dear friend of mine. He has had some misfortune at his estate in Wiltshire. Bloody place has been burned down; costing him a fortune to build it. But old William has pots of money which is mainly generated by his plantations in Jamaica. Trouble is, the French are attacking merchant ships from here to the West Indies, and no one wants the job. But I told him that I know a man who may have the guts for it.'

He raised his eyebrows and his glass for me to clink in agreement. I had walked straight into his hands when I had asked to purchase land, and he knew it. The venture was a risky one, and I did not much like the idea of being killed at sea or back in a French prison once again. What he was asking however would be worth the risk, only if I could negotiate suitable terms for my efforts.

I raised my glass and smiled back.

'I assume the man who goes to collect this cargo would make a tidy sum from the inflated sugar prices sir,' I asked in way of telling him that I would need to be well compensated, even with the half-priced land he was selling me.

'You would assume correctly. In addition to that, you may trade in your usual fashion on the outbound journey; to make it even more worthwhile. You will also have my thanks, and that of my friend who was the Sherriff of London not long ago, a position of great benefit to a man in your profession Mr Carter,' he said, and walked me over to a globe map. As he spun it around to examine it, I gave him the answer he wanted.

I wanted the world and all its bounty. The rich men such as Lord Arundell and his friends, had inherited their outrageous wealth. I had inherited nothing from my father, God rest his soul.

'I am your man my Lord,' I said to him, as he looked up from the globe beaming at my agreement. 'Splendid... how soon can you depart man?' he asked eagerly. In truth, I didn't know, but I couldn't tell him that. 'I would say around three months or so sir.'

'I need to make some arrangements first,' I added. He nodded in agreement and pointed to the map.

'The sugar is at a warehouse in Kingston. I will dispatch letters of introduction to his man there, informing him of your arrival. I take it you have never been to the West Indies before Carter?'

'I have not sir. But I will assemble a crew that has. It will be a good experience for me.'

'Good man, that's the spirit. Oh, by the way. The sugar you are transporting will have to be brought into London docks, and the normal tax duty must be paid. We can't have Williams good name tarnished you see. He would be horrified to know I had commissioned someone with your expertise. But anything outbound, as I have said, is your business.'

'I will make arrangements immediately sir. Thank you for intrusting me with this cargo, I won't let you or your friend down.'

'I know you will not Carter, now let's save the boring arrangements until after supper. You will dine with us of course?' he asked. 'I would be honoured sir; most honoured.'

'Good, good; I'm going to set me wife onto you now Mr Carter. I do apologise for her bluntness, but she is a curious creature.'

The feast that the Arundell's had displayed on the table, was something only from my wildest imagination and dreams. Upon the large mahogany table was a cloth of the most intricate lace, and on top of that were plates of various meats and local vegetables. Everything had been prepared with great pomp and magnificence, and I did not believe that they had done so just on my behalf.

I even asked the Lady Arundell this question. 'Oh no… we always eat this way. I am glad you like it… Now tell me about your time in France Mr Carter,' she asked excitedly.

One of the servants poured some wine and I helped myself to a large helping of pheasant and rabbit. It must have been how the King of Prussia dined, I mused at the time.

I told them in animated detail about my adventures as a smuggling man. I left the odd moment out but was quite forthright. Lord Arundell would have been informed anyway, so I let my natural storytelling ability sweep them away like one of the characters from their extensive library.

We were classes apart, but by the end of the evening I spoke to them both like old friends. They invited me to stay the night, to which I accepted readily. The bed, like the rest of their home was something extraordinary. The mattress on the four-poster bed was so soft; it felt as if I had slept in the clouds.

In the morning, breakfast was brought into my room, and I decided that I could get used to that kind of treatment very easily. I did not want to outstay my welcome though, and I was very aware that I had a great deal of arrangements to put in place for the voyage to Jamaica, as well as ensuring the stability and consistency of my other business.

My French contraband for example was flowing well, and the wool and coin going to Lieutenant Domenici was in steady streams, pleasing him immensely.

So, I bid the Arundell's farewell and thanked them for their hospitality. I left on old Francis my steed, and accompanied by Mr Treluddra, who had proven to be good company on the long ride home.

I had come to buy land, and I had done that for half its value. I had also made a good friend of Lord Arundell and his wife, who had given me a fine cargo to collect in new territories overseas. The Lord once again had decided to reward me. I was now an owner of land, small though it was, but owner never the less. Prussia Cove, Bessie Cove and Pixy Cove were now mine, as well as the farm where my mother, and family still dwelt.

I had hoped my father would've been proud of his eldest son. One day we'll meet again, and I may ask him.

CHAPTER 18

I told my mother the news that we owned the farm outright. She rejoiced and wept at the providence. We had lived a hard and poor life before and owning the farm would give the Carter family certain independence.

My brother Francis; now a young man, had found a love of God, and any spare time not working on the farm, he spent with his nose in a Bible or at our nearest church. I loved how Harry, my other brother, chased him around and pestered him to play war games, only to be rejected by Francis, who was more interested in his studies.

I asked Francis if he would like to join the cove boys and work for me. But he refused out of hand. He had a different path in mind, and even at such a young age, he looked down on my profession.

I could not help but love him more at the time for his devotion. I feared God like the next man. But I had my dreams and kept my own council on such affairs. Harry would later become both the perfect smuggler and devoted Methodist. He would be just as

The King of Prussia Cove

famous in Cornwall as I was becoming, but his story is for another book perhaps.

I had so much to prepare for, and I needed a ship and a crew with experience, and courage enough to sail the dangerous waters we would be venturing into. Fortunately, with the help of the Tonkin family, it did not take long to find good men. Uriah Tonkin was running to be Mayor of Penzance the following year. With his support from my friends and the patronage of Lord Arundell, he stood a good chance to win in the following May elections. He was much older than John Tonkin but no less charismatic. I got on with him straight away, and we spoke at length about my voyage to Jamaica. I told him I would make it my business to ensure he won a victory against the Borlace family, who were also in and out of the Mayoral seat, as much as the Tonkin's were.

He introduced me to some of his friends who had worked for the West Indian Company, and to a man named Henry Diggins, who had been a lieutenant on one of the companies' ships which used to frequent the Caribbean. He was keen to join me, and even knew some lads who also wanted the chance to earn some decent coin.

The West Indian ships were still trading out of the West Indies. But more and more cargoes were becoming lost to the predatory French, who stalked the waters like sharks looking for their next meal.

This was why William Beckford needed privateers like me to increase the distribution of one of the most valuable items sought on the market, which was sugar. The commodity, once only available to the wealthy aristocracy, had become affordable to even the common man, due to the increased output of production. This increase in production however was due to the many plantations that had risen from the Caribbean islands, to compete with the cotton and Tobacco being grown in North American Virginia. But more so, thanks to the multitude of Negro slaves from Africa.

I had never seen a Negro before, but I was told they were simple and strong, which made them the perfect labour force to work the plantations and cotton fields. I would later be proved wrong about those poor Africans, who were as intelligent and resourceful as any white man. I have become friends with many black men and women in my life. But as usual, I am skipping ahead again.

With my crew ready, I only had to acquire a ship suitable to make the journey. We purchased a large fourth rate vessel with twenty guns called The Atlas. An apt name for the weight it would soon carry. We had purchased it together with the Tonkin's, and I hoped it would make my fortune. James, my partner, would have been better placed to run our business from Prussia Cove. I needed a good man there. But he begged to come with me. He had always wanted to see the Americas and West Indies, and I could not refuse him, so passionate was his plea to come.

I left the affairs of the cove to Charles and trusted him to keep things moving well. William Vingoe was now serving the Admiralty on a large cutter called the Wolf. He was terrorising all the enemies of the British Empire and making quite a name for himself. I asked his father John Vingoe if he could help me out and send over some of his lads to bolster my cove boys, and made sure distribution continued while I was away.

I asked Samuel the poacher if he would come with us, and fight if the need ever arose. He was reluctant at first. Not because of the fighting of course. He loved to do that. It was the time away at sea that concerned him the most. Eventually he agreed when I offered him a large cut of the profits. The one percent he would make pleased him no end.

We were all but ready to sail. But I had one more person to say farewell to. I had been dreading it.

Summoning courage, I made the journey to see my wife Marie. She knew what I did and would never bat an eyelid when I made a trip to France and Guernsey, she understood the dangers and the risks I faced. I didn't know how she would respond when I told her I would be away for a long while. I didn't know when I would be back. But it would surely be many months before I would see her sweet face again.

'You will miss the birth of your child John,' she said to me simply.

It was true that I would miss it. When Lord Arundell asked me to go, my unborn child and wife had been on my mind greatly. But what could I say? I wanted to buy the very land that my children and their children could inherit, long after my passing. I had to agree. This was my life, and she would have to accept it.

'I will miss it Marie, that is true; but I do this for both of you. I promised myself once that I would never be poor. My father died poor and broken. I will not, and neither will you if I do well on this voyage. I am collecting for a Member of Parliament Marie, a former Sherriff of London no less,' I said to her with pain in my heart. She nodded and could not hold back the tears which were hard to watch fall.

'I am just being silly. Of course, you must go... I will pray for your safe return John,' she said, and kissed me passionately. I savoured that kiss with my love Marie, and we parted very emotionally.

***

We set out soon after, and all the excitement we felt evaporated after the first days on the choppy Atlantic Ocean. I had my sea legs, as did most of the crew, but even those used to sailing experienced an element of seasickness. Samuel The Poacher had been tirelessly sick over the guardrail, and James patted his back in between being sick himself. It was after four days of rough sailing when the sea became calm enough to take any kind of enjoyment from our journey. Samuel practiced with his bow, and even missed a few targets before becoming accustomed to the movement of the deck.

I had filled our hold to the brim with claret, which I had purchased with Cornish wool. I would smuggle the claret to Boston, where I was to find a gentleman named Mr Jackson, who I was told would buy any wine or spirits that a merchant brought into the country.

We encountered no enemy ships on our outward voyage and landed in Boston to be met by the harbour master, and several soldiers who pocked around our ship like a pack of hungry dogs. They then inspected my papers from Lord Arundell and were satisfied that I had nothing of interest. Nothing was found on the ship of course.

I had become an expert at concealing contraband and it was no less of a challenge to fool the authorities in America than it was back in Britain.

I found the address of Mr Jackson and made my deal for the wine.

'The fighting here has made anything worth drinking hard to get hold of Mr Carter,' he told me once we had shaken on an agreed amount. What he told me had been true. I tried to buy a drink in a nearby tavern and was shocked by the price. America, it seemed, were suffering worse than my own country.

In times of war, I would always work harder than ever; knowing that a period of conflict would place my goods in high demand.

The seven years' war with France was becoming my first experience of these inflated prices; and like any good businessman, I made sure I was always there to fill the gap in the market.

We unloaded our goods under the cover of night; the bottles of claret were placed in a cart, and then covered in straw to conceal them from the less than vigilant soldiers. I had given them some money earlier that day and assumed that they would take it. They were not paid well by the crown and would take a bribe as readily as a squirrel seeing a nut in the open.

My claret was gone in a matter of hours, and I had made double the amount of what I could have sold it for in England.

I told my men to enjoy the towns drinking establishments, including any dens of sin to satisfy some of their lustful desires. I thanked God that I had no such desires to be quenched in that fashion and decided to avoid those places. I had some money to spend however and distracted myself in other ways while on land.

Boston was a vibrant place with paved roads to the most part, and I walked past a leather goods store, noticing the man working within was a negro. I entered intent on buying a belt and new coat for the cold days and nights at sea. I had expected the man to be dim witted and difficult to strike a bargain with.

I always liked to make a deal you see, no matter what I was buying or selling.

'Excuse me; is there anyone who can help me purchase one of those fine coats hanging up,' I said to him, not entirely sure he would comprehend a word I was saying. I had seen plenty of black men around the dock, but this was the first one I had spoken with.

'There's no one here but me sir, but I can help you with anything you need,' he replied kindly, smiling perfect white teeth. I did not see the harm in it, so asked the price of a few items, and then started bartering gently with the man. We struck a deal on very agreeable terms, and I slipped a bottle of claret into the bargain for his owner, who arrived once the deal was done.

'Good afternoon sir, I trust Mr Hall has accommodated to your needs?' he inquired and patted his slave on the back as if they were colleagues. 'He has sir, thank you. He runs a hard bargain,' I replied. 'I've taught him everything I know; he's a slave, but the damn finest worker of leather I did ever see… Prince I'm off for the evening. Make sure you lock up... Good day sir,' he said to me before leaving once again.

'He treats you well then?' I asked Mr Hall.

He looked up and smiled again. 'Oh, he treats me very well sir; better than most coloured folk around here.' He replied.

I spoke to him about England, and he was very enthusiastic to hear what it was like there. I noticed suddenly that we had been speaking for a long time, without realising I had been conversing with a man equal to my intellect and charisma.

I was my own man in life, and still am to this day. If a man tells me the sky is blue, then I would look up and make up my own mind on the matter. I decided in that moment that black people could be men of intelligence, and I would treat them as such.

'So, will you be going home soon Mr Carter sir?' he asked.

'I have one more stop to make… I'm headed for Jamaica to transport a quantity of sugar back to London.'

He seemed to freeze at the mention of Jamaica, and I asked if he was alright.

'That's a merciless place sir; I was sold there to Mr O'Brian, many years ago. I still have the scars on my back from that wicked place. I hear the plantations are getting bigger and bigger too,' he said with such sadness.

I was concerned about going to Jamaica, but I would judge the place with my own eyes when I got there.

It had been a pleasant experience meeting Mr Hall, and I told him if ever I returned to Boston, I would come and see him again. I shook his hand and bedded down for the night in a nearby inn.

I liked Boston. It was a busy place of commerce, and I could tell it was a prime location for trade.

Before I left, I made some enquiries to rent some warehouses to store future goods in. I planned to service this country with imported goods both legally, and by way of smuggling. Their taxes were even harsher than ours after all.

The King was spending a large sum to fund the French Indian war, and the colonists would have to pay for it through the high taxation of goods. I could once again see opportunity beckoning and agreed to rent a small warehouse close to the docks. I made arrangements for an agent to purchase cotton and tobacco and store it within those warehouses. Later, I would replace it with gin, brandy and wine, when I returned here once again.

CHAPTER 19

When we left Boston docks, the waters were calm, almost tranquil. The wind was gentle, yet still gave the Atlas's sails enough push to make good speed. The crew had been well rested and were in good spirits as we made our way south towards the Caribbean. I chose to stay close to the American coast, for two reasons. The first was my curiosity. We had maps a plenty, but I wanted to get to know the many nooks and crannies the coastline offered for smuggling goods. The other reason was the weather. If we got into any difficulties, there were a multitude of rivers and natural harbours which we could shelter in. The only risk was the French warships stalking the coastline, as were the British ships.

We came across our first spot of danger not long after we left Boston docks.

In the distance I could just make out a ship, but it was impossible to see if it was a friend or foe. It must have spotted our sails also, as it turned towards us fast. I prepared the men for action, and Samuel The Poacher lined up his wicked armaments on the deck, like a collection of tradesman's tools. I made sure my men manned the small compliment of twenty guns we had on board, and the rest stood nervously with loaded muskets, and a pouch full of shot. I hoped we would not have to use them.

'Are they French?' someone shouted. I strained my eyes. Then with dismay I realised the flag being flown from their mast was indeed the enemy. The French had us in their sights and I found it most difficult to summon my courage.

I paced up and down the deck with my chin held high to lend the men some measure of composure which I did not feel in all honesty. Mr Diggin our ship's Captain brought a measurable amount of order, shouting commands and sending men into the rigging to unfurl sails.

'We're going to run for it Mr Carter. We cannot compete with a foe such as that,' he told me under his breath, so as not to be overheard by the men. 'Can we outrun them?' I asked him hopefully.

'We can… just about anyway. It's just as well we have no cargo on board, or we'd be doomed.' He gave orders to make as best speed possible, away from our pursuers through the churning waves swelling so large, the distant French ship bobbed in and out of sight.

They had over double the number of guns that we had, and I decided there and then that if we did not make a dash from the predator, it would have surly blown us out of the water.

We could not hope to survive a battle with the French ship, which bore down on us slowly and intently.

Luckily for us, our Captain, Mr Diggin was an extraordinary sailor. He and the crew knew these waters like I knew the Cornish coastline. He brought The Atlas close to shore and skirted around the rocks poking up menacingly out of the water. I looked at them with terror as the waves crashed against them, causing a salty spray to moisten our faces on deck.

If the Captain missed a rock formation, then our ship would've been smashed to pieces. I felt helpless, and all I could do was watch and pray.

In the twilight of the evening, it was dangerous to flirt so brazenly in unfamiliar waters. We had all seen the wrecks back home, where survival was rare when the sea was as violent as it was that day.

'Rocks ahead Captain!' screamed Samuel The Poacher, whose keen eyes picked out the dark and foreboding doom before us.

Captain Diggin ordered a swift turn to starboard and the ship lurched to an impossible angle, nearly sending my partner James overboard. I held onto the rigging for my life and reached out just in time to save him from a watery grave.

The ship, now clear of danger, steadied out as we gathered our balance once more. In the distance behind the French warship, I could see the sky darkening, quicker than it should have at dusk.

A storm was brewing, and in no time, overtook us both, making our endeavour thrice more dangerous.

The French ship, frustrated with the possibility of losing us, fired a broadside from their cannon which hit the frothing sea harmlessly. As if in retaliation the sea struck back and pushed our pursuer ever closer to the razor-sharp rocks.

'She's hit, she's hit,' whooped Samuel elated. 'My God, I think your right; set course out to sea, into the storm man. We don't want to end up sharing her fate,' the Captain responded, taking the small telescope from Samuel, eager to see our enemy left behind. It had been a dangerous tactic to sail among the craggy coastline. But if we had not done so, then we would have been easy prey for the French to devour at their leisure. The weather had helped somewhat.

But we had to count ourselves lucky that day. The threat had been real and way too close for comfort.

CHAPTER 20

'What's that smell?' Samuel asked as we approached the docks at Kingston. The warm climate had been a welcomed boon when we came into the tranquil Caribbean waters. The air was humid, and the sun baked our skins red as lobsters in a boiling brew.

Other ships bound from Africa had arrived with us, and where a stone's throw away, when we were all forced to hold our noses.

'That there is a slave ship me lad. You will not smell it's like if you live a thousand years,' Captain Diggin informed me, and helped himself to pickled herring and salted beef from our stores. I could not eat a thing with that stench, as the slave ship drew in close alongside us.

We both docked in the harbour, and I watched in horror as hundreds of sore ridden wretches emerged from the lower decks of the slaver in chains.

They wore iron collars and had eyes like the walking dead. The slave masters then whipped them along the gangplank and into pens.

With great reluctance they hobbled along in their confines, like broken cattle awaiting slaughter. The cargos of human meat were not to be killed though.

No… They were far too valuable for that. Those doomed men were the Black Negro men of Africa; now destined for a life of servitude, and no better than working animals of burden.

I have always counted myself as an independent thinker, and right from the outset I knew it was wrong.

In those days, as it still is today, slavery was rife, and a man could profit tremendously from the commodity of man flesh. That's what they were; men.

They were a different colour yes. But they were men, and one of Gods creations. I would not have treated a stubborn beast the way those poor fellows were being abused. One black man had tried to launch himself into the water. Only to be stopped by a vigilant slaver who detached him from the rest, and led him roughly to a waggon wheel, which had been placed at the harbour for that cruel purpose.

The man then tied him onto the wheel and turned him upside down. Without stopping for ceremony, he pulled his whip and began swinging, lash after lash, until the Negros back was shredded to ribbons. The crimson blood dripped at first. Then ran like a stream, which pooled on the sandy ground beneath him.

'My God… I have never seen such barbarism,' I said to some of the lads who gathered to watch the bizarre spectacle.

'It's how our sugar and many other luxuries are acquired. It's sad to witness, but a necessary evil I'm afraid,' the Captain said without compassion.

'Have you ever worked on a slaving ship sir?' I asked him, incredulous that so many Christian men could deem this treatment as necessary.

'I have not Mr Carter. I haven't the stomach for it. But the fact remains, without the slaves, the British Empire would lose a fortune in wealth. As would many men,' he answered, convinced with his reasoning.

He was correct in a way, but I was disgusted by what I was witnessing. The screams of the slave being whipped to with an inch of his life were becoming weaker and weaker. He started to grunt, as he accepted the pain. Then suddenly, he passed into unconsciousness. The lashes then stopped, and he was cut down, landing hard into a bloody heap.

No help of aid came his way, and when the last of the Negros passed into the waiting pens, bent up and twisted from the long voyage, his body was added to the others who had died so terribly.

The pile of death was the last straw for me. I turned and headed into the nearest tavern to drink myself stupid, and attempt to remove the horror, now engrained upon my memory.

'The smell lingers around the whole bloody place then,' Samuel piped up with his nose wrinkled with distaste. I had been in blissful ignorance to the plight and injustice towards the black men of Africa.

'Let's just get the sugar we came for and go. I will not stay here for any longer than I have to,' I whispered to Samuel and James, who both shared my table. I had not spoken quietly enough, because a rough and viscous looking man a table away piped up.

'Don't you like this paradise boy? I thought you and your crew looked simple when you walked in here.' At his table were three men who were equally as sinister as the one who had spoken. Pirates I was told frequented the islands and by the look of the other customers in the tavern, we had walked straight into the dragon's mouth.

I could have backed down meekly, but I had learned early on that strength should be met with strength. They would tear a man limb from limb if they displayed any weakness.

'I'm having a private conversation with my fellows,' I said, trying to portray an air of grandeur and dominance. We were all big men, and armed to the teeth, so I hoped my confidence would dissuade him from any lethal confrontation. 'You would be wise not to make such remarks again,' I said evenly. Samuel had stood from his chair as soon as the man had started to speak ill to us. No one paid him heed, thinking he was moving away to avoid any trouble.

The men at the table all stood, with the leader pulling a half moon dagger from a hidden scabbard. The evening was getting late, and in the candle light the blades wicked edge gleamed menacingly.

He then held its keen point towards me aiming at my face. 'You talk big for a young whippersnapper. Let's see how tough you are when I cut your ears and nose off eh,' the man said gruffly to James and me, with murderous hate in his bloodshot eyes. Too much rum in some men did not agree with their tempers. This man had clearly been looking for a fight; and after what we had just witnessed at the docks, he would find one.

I had been in a dark mood and recognised one of the men with him as the man who had whipped the poor Negro to death on the wagon wheel.

Before I could vent my fury upon the villainous scoundrels, Samuel came out of the shadows like a wrath in the night. He struck one of the men over the head so hard with the butt of his pistol, that the crack made the whole tavern still and silent.

Slowly he pulled back the hammers on both of his drawn pistols, and calmly placed the barrels against the temples of each man.

The attack had come out of nowhere, and the instigator with the knife, stood there dumb and wide eyed at his sudden misfortune.

Because of our youth, they had assumed we were wet behind the ears. But the slavers had misjudged us in their drunken stupor.

'I'll blow a great big hole in both ya skulls if you don't drop that knife. I think I would enjoy that… Wouldn't you like to see that John?' Samuel said gruffly.

Now standing, we loomed over the small trouble makers, for Sam and I were tall, powerfully built young men in our prime. The slavers swallowed in unison at their foolish error of judgement. No one came to help them, which emboldened me to give them a taste of their own medicine. I hated bullies. The Ferret had been a bully, as had his masters the Godolphin's. That was perhaps why he had joined the customs men, who were just as loathsome as he was.

The men before us had picked a very unfortunate time to harass me, and I revelled in that moment God forgive me.

'I would like to see that Samuel. A small piece of justice I would say, for what he did earlier.' I pointed to the man who had lashed the slave to death. 'Oh… you're not one those black lovers are ye?' he said without thinking of his predicament.

I would not entertain them with my philosophy of the correct treatment of all men. So, I just shook my head, feeling a fury building up inside of me.

Samuel prodded them in the head to emphasise the point that he had loaded pistols ready to fire. It was enough to make the man drop the blade and sneer at me in frustrated defeat.

He spat tobacco on the wooden floor, nearly covering my boots with a dark brown gob. I could have let Samuel carryout his threat in that moment. But I had a better idea to teach them a lesson, as well as air out my frustrations.

'Outside then, if you think you can teach me a lesson,' I said to the one who held the knife. The place erupted into excitement, and he rolled up his shirt sleeves in answer, and headed for the door. Wagers were being placed before we had even made it outside, and a square of men formed in gleeful anticipation for a bit of sport in the humid evening at the docks.

Some gentlemen and soldiers came over to join the crowed, but instead of breaking us up, they began to make their own wagers, and all eyes were on the fiend and me.

James had taken some action on our behalf.

He knew how well I could box a man's ears. He had seen me do it back home.

Samuel holstered his pistols but kept his hands on them to discourage any further foul play.

'I beat the black animals every day lad; you will be no different. You should have just walked out of here while you had the chance,' he laughed, not believing his luck at getting the chance to thrash me. Latter I would find out that while in Jamaica, he had always started trouble of some description. By all accounts he was known to be a viscous fighter, and most locals gave him a wide berth when he was around, especially when drinking. Of course, I was ignorant to that, and squared up to him without fear of his reputation.

The crowd cheered, and I moved towards him, ready to throw a testing jab at his unprotected jaw. He had no guard up whatsoever, and as I threw the weak punch, he rolled away on the floor, and unseen by me, picked up a handful of sand. When I came at him again he threw the fistful of it at my eyes, momentarily blinding me.

I had never faced such a dirty fighter before, but in those opening moments I realised that he was very dirty indeed.

He made good advantage of my temporary blindness and hit me hard on my own jaw, loosening a tooth, but causing little damage to me. I rode the punch by turning with it, always moving and bobbing like a barrel in the sea. I made myself an impossible target for him to get another solid punch.

He attacked my groin with a kick, and I jumped back and danced around him, desperately trying to protect my manhood.

My eyes were watering but gradually my vision returned. They were uncomfortable to say the least, but it was my turn to lay on some punishment.

I did not need any foul play to win that battle, and with my whole body, I pounced on him and grasped his shirt with my vice like grip. My other hand was balled into a fist, which found its mark at the base of his nose.

The bone gave way exploding into a shower of blood and snot.

I drew my arm back again to round house the vermin, and end the fight quickly; instinctively, he put his arm up to fend off the telegraphed blow, but it did not do him any good. The ferocity of the attack blew through his feeble resistance, and knocked him onto his backside, sliding towards the ever-pressing crowd of bystanders. I was impressed that he had not been rendered unconscious from my wild punch.

It must have dawned on him though, that the young whippersnapper was more than his match.

One of his friends knelt next to him and placed another dagger into his hand. But I saw the danger this time, and as he tried to gain his feet from his knees, I kicked him as hard as I could, letting out all my frustrations in a last and final strike, snapping his head back and ending the fight in an instant.

When he eventually woke up, he would have a severe headache. His friends losing their bravery shrank away into the mass of people, not wanting to get involved after watching their ringleader dispatched so effortlessly.

James picked up the knife from the floor where the downed man had dropped it after my kick.

'Come on John; let's get you out of here and to bed,' James said over the roaring cheers of the onlookers. I was patted on the back for my triumph, and then I too slipped away to find suitable lodging for the night. After so long at sea, a good solid bed that didn't move was most welcome.

'Thank you for your help lads,' I said to my friends.

Samuel winked at me. 'What are friends for, besides, how are we going to get paid if you get yourself killed?' He jabbed me playfully as James located our lodgings.

I have never slept so well in all my life than I did that night. All thought of slavery, battles at sea and fighting were swallowed into oblivion. The rum I had consumed may have been partly responsible for my delightfully long dreamless sleep.

When I did eventually open my eyes, one thought nagged me. I was missing home.

Marie would have given birth to our child by now, and I felt an immense compulsion to see them both.

But I was the other side of the world, and I would have to finish what I had agreed to. Men are made by reputation you see. One thing people had always associated with me was my reliability. If I made a deal I would stick to it. My word was my bond and I would see the job through.

CHAPTER 21

The next day we kept a low profile, not wanting any more trouble than necessary. We were to contact a man name John Pinney and make arrangements to load William Beckford's sugar onto The Atlas.

We found Mr Beckford's agent in a nearby warehouse and I introduced myself to the man who ran the sugar plantations and slaves on the former Sherriff of London's behalf.

'Good day sir; my name is John Carter. I have instructions to transport some of Mr Beckford's refined sugar. Here are my papers for your perusal.' I had lightened up somewhat after the fight from the previous night. My fame had ensured I was already known to him, and Mr Pinney shook my hand eagerly. Even for a master of slaves, it was difficult not to like the man.

'Oh, thank goodness, we've so much in our stores we can't get it back to London fast enough. I must say that was an extremely entertaining bout last night. I won a tidy sum on you… What a punch man, what a punch indeed.'

He examined my papers and decided quickly that the stamped document with Beckford's seal was in order. 'I hope you don't mind sir, but I would like to conclude business as fast as possible and make good time for our journey home,' I said, attempting to appeal to his sense of haste to get his product out from under his feet. The larger than life character was having none of it though.

'Nonsense Mr Carter, you must dine with me tonight and fill me in on all the gossip back in England. I won't take no for an answer.' I smiled and agreed reluctantly. I had supposed that after the long voyage to get there, one night more wouldn't hurt.

'Very well sir,' I replied politely.

'Excellent; we can go over the loading details tonight also,' he said.

'In the meantime, let my man here take you around the warehouse eh.'

His man was a very large and muscular Negro, who wore a white wig, and was dressed far better than most of the other poor souls I had seen on the island.

He led me to where the crates were waiting to be collected, and I was not sure if the black man spoke any English. The ones coming off the slave ships had communicated in their African dialect, but when he introduced himself, he spoke perfect and cultured English, without a trace of an accent whatsoever.

His name was Philip, and I attempted to talk to him, just as I had done with Mr Hall the leather store worker back in Boston. 'Thank you for showing me around. How long have you been in Mr Pinney's service if you don't mind me asking?'

'Since I was a child sir; I used to work in the fields, but I was fortunate enough to be able to serve the master personally.'

'I can see why that would be better.' I replied to him sadly. I tried to talk further of his plight, which was a difficult task. He was very polite, but years in servitude had made him naturally cautious of his white masters.

After examining the cargo, he showed me to a house which was built onto the side of the warehouse. Inside the place were fine rugs and paintings on the wall, rich mahogany furniture and porcelain figurines dotted here and there.

The house was lavished in all the trappings of wealth and I suspected that without the slaves that wealth would all but dry up.

I was given a tour of the house and told its brief history, which did not span too many years. The British Empire after all had not been there that long, but already had begun to transform its landscape and population.

'You must see my tailor Mr Carter; I'll warrant you are sick of wearing seaman's cloths for months on end. He's the best in the West Indies, and remarkably cheaper than the ones back home,' Mr Pinney said extravagantly when Phillip and I returned.

'Thank you, sir, but that is quite all right. I am comfortable enough in what I have on,' I said without embarrassment. I had worked hard to acquire the decent cloths I had. In truth, I loved to dress in the finery of the gentry. But I would have lost the respect of the lads if I had strutted around like a peacock.

'Nonsense man; I can't very well dine with you looking like that. Come sir, enjoy yourself.' The comment should have offended me, but he said it in such a way that made you laugh along with him. I had tried to dislike the man, for he was a slave master. But his flamboyance and good humour was infections.

'Very well sir. I assume it would be impossible to protest,' I stated mildly. He looked down at himself and bowed flamboyantly to me.

'You will thank me for it later, I'm sure Mr Carter.'

My intention was to visit the tailor briefly. But once inside, I was fussed over, and treated like a lord of the land. Fredrick of Prussia and King George himself could not have wished for better service.

Captain Diggin had come with me but asked politely to miss the dinner with Pinney. He did not say why, and I did not push him on the subject.

The tailor was named Mr Clark, and he was just as eccentric as my new friend John Pinney. They were almost effeminate in a way.

I had heard about such men, but as they say, ignorance is bliss. I did not wish to find out if they were inclined in such ways. But I could not help but enjoy their entertaining behaviour.

After several hours of fussing, I wore the best set of cloths I had ever owned.

Captain Diggin looked just as good in a brown suit he had been fitted with.

I had chosen a cream suit of clothes, a new white shirt and cravat. All I needed now was a fitting pair of shoes and decent hat to match.

We had money to spend, Diggin and the wine we had sold in Boston had brought in a tremendous amount of money. Our profits from the sugar, which we would bring back, would only add to our increasing wealth further. When we were shown the best sets of shoes made from top quality leather, we bought them without shame or hesitation. The hats we purchased cost enough to feed a poor family back home for months, but we had taken Mr Pinney's advice, and were starting to enjoy ourselves. After the near disasters getting here, and the possible risks from the French on our return to England, we both thought it wise to spoil ourselves.

I also bought some petticoats and pretty dresses for Marie. But I didn't know what to buy my new child, because unfortunately I had no knowledge on whether I had a son or daughter waiting for me back home. So, I did not buy any cloths for the little one. Instead I found a rattle, and a neatly carved toy horse. I could not wait to see them.

But first I had a job to do.

The dinner was set for seven o'clock, and I arrived promptly, such was my way.

Philip, his black slave, led me to the dining room where Mr Pinney waited for me, brandy in hand.

'Hello Mr Carter, you look splendid. Well, don't you feel better now you're in some damn fine cloths eh?' he boomed, and came to shake my hand energetically. 'You were right sir, I do feel good... I enjoyed it actually,' I replied honestly.

'I knew you would… Come; let's eat, and you can fill me in about news from home.' he said, taking a seat at the table, which was full of plates with silver covers.

Philip removed the lids and steam wafted up, making my mouth water greedily.

The food which had been prepared was even more stupendous as the Arundell feast. There were tropical birds, with parts of their feathers remaining on their tails for decoration. Roasted piglets and sides of beef that were drizzled in a sweet sauce; I could have been dinning in heaven.

The wine was just as good, and I spoke at length about my journey and the events back in England. He listened with great interest, and it was clear that he missed the old country, even though he lived so well in the West Indies. I asked him if he liked living in Jamaica, and he confirmed my suspicions.

'I want for nothing Mr Carter, but it can get frightfully hot out here. The bugs can be a pain in the arse as well I can tell you,' he informed me, with dramatic misery.

'But it is not without its pleasures of course,' he added merrily.
'Of course,' I agreed.

The evening was an enjoyable one, and Philip his slave, catered to our every need. He brought out candies after our meal, and I scoffed them down, enjoying the sweet tastes that lingered long after our meal. We spoke little of business, for we had made most of the transportation arrangements earlier in the day at the warehouse. The goods were to be loaded by his inexhaustible supply of Negro's, who would ensure my hold was filled to the brim with sugar by the following day.

We eventually retired to his library. But it was not a patch on the Arundell's extensive collection. I was still impressed with it none the less.

He did not read much, and only kept a library because most gentlemen did. He then invited me to help myself to my choice of books for the long voyage home. I accepted readily and chose some poetry books and books with adventure in them.

I thanked him and then asked him a question that had been nagging at me since I first stepped foot in Jamaica. 'I hope you don't find this rude, but I'd like to ask you a question about the slaves here.' My intention was not to offend him, but I normally spoke my mind, and I felt compelled to do so.

'Yes. You may ask,' he nodded sympathetically, as if he knew what I would say.

'I just wanted to know if you agree with how they are treated. When we arrived, we saw some ghastly sights that will no doubt haunt me for the rest of my days.'

Unfortunately, as I sit all these years later, my word that day had proven true. I remember it so vividly. The smells and the screams were burned into my memory like a curse. The thing I would remember most, more than anything else, was the blood.

'When I first came here Mr Carter, I was just as shocked and appalled as you are now. But living here for so long, you come to realise that our way of life could not exist if not for the sale and ownership of human flesh.' He looked over at his house slave with no shame and pointed at him to help me understand.

'Take Philip here. He lives a very good life, has food and shelter, as do they all. Most live better lives than the poor wretches in England.'

I could see what he was trying to say. I just could not except that a son of God, no matter what colour of his skin, could be used in such a manner.

Maybe it was because I had felt like a slave once, when I worked down the mines, pulling tin from the ground for my masters above.

Or maybe it was the fact that I had spent a good deal of time in a French prison and knew the misery of losing my liberty.

'I can see that Philip wants for little sir. But why do they treat them so savagely, why torture them? I saw a man whipped to death for trying to escape, before I had even made landfall. Surly you see this as wrong. I would not treat a beast like that,' I reasoned.

He nodded, and I was relieved he did not take my questioning the wrong way.

'I do not treat them like some men do Mr Carter. I have a gentle nature and try to treat them well. Some must be punished. That is sometimes unavoidable. I would not terrorise the poor fellows though, but you must understand that the world as we know it would not exist, if not for the labour force of the slaves. Now, let's not talk of such dark topics, and enjoy some more brandy eh,' he concluded neatly changing the subject.

I wanted to argue my case and try and convince him of his wickedness. But no matter what I felt, he and the system would not change.

We drank our brandies, and I left very late that night.

Mr Pinney begged me to stay the night in his house, but I wisely refused his offer. I walked for the door, and instead of shaking my hand, he leaned in and tried to kiss me goodbye.

My instinct was to sock him on his jaw. But I gave him the benefit of doubt that he could have just been a blind drunkard confusing me for a lady. I was still very young and naive at the time and would not have guessed that he preferred the company of gentlemen in all respects. I managed to escape fortunately, shouting my thanks down the street, not sure if he would remember my swift exit in the morning.

When I returned to our lodgings, the lads roared with laughter, and Captain Diggin told me the real reason why he did not go for dinner with Pinney.

'I've been to this island many times John,' he told me. 'One time he invited me to dinner the same way he did to you. A likable man I might add. But he only likes the company of men if you catch my meaning,' he explained awkwardly.

Some of the crew went into further detail and I was glad I had made it out when I did. I did not mind Mr Pinney being the way he was. He was too likable a character for that. If ever I was asked again to dinner by the man, I would more than likely still go. Only next time, I would vastly limit the amount we drank.

CHAPTER 22

The next day I awoke early to supervise the loading of the ship, ensuring we collected the maximum amount we could possibly carry. I allowed myself and the lads a short while to enjoy being on land, when everything was in readiness to leave for home.

It would be a most profitable venture, and that was partly due to the wine I had smuggled into Boston.

The night before we left Jamaica, I explored the island around the coast. I wanted to see its beauty before the British swallowed it up with industry and profiteering.

I was glad I did venture into the wild, for my opinion of the place changed dramatically, as I took in the sun setting over distant horizon. The beach was like powder, and I took off my boots to enjoy the cool grains of sand wash over my feet like silk. I paddled in the shallows of the blue tranquil waters, and watched seabirds take flight from my approach.

Since those adventurous days, I have seen many wondrous things on my travels, but that moment alone on the beach of Jamaica, I experienced a moment of utter peace.

The King of Prussia Cove

Taking off my cloths, I stood naked as the day I was born and bathed in the warm water that had been too inviting to resist. Tiny fish of all the colours of the rainbow swam around me, and I thought that I may have been too quick in saying that I would not return to this magical place.

Such was man's way, to corrupt and spoil the marvels of this world. My serene thoughts were instantly washed away however when I heard a branch break in the treeline of the jungle. I snapped my head up, and was more worried about being seen stark naked, than encountering any threat. I did not know if they had any wild animals on the island, and I rushed to my cloths before I could find out.

As I reached the area where I had disrobed, the mystery of the branch breaking was made known.

A loud crack of gunpowder ignited, and I felt the air whistle by my face. The musket shot had been so close in fact, that the heat from the projectile singed my clean-shaven cheek.

I was unharmed, and acutely aware I had no weapon to fend off the shooter, who could have loaded at their leisure to take another shot at me.

My only option was to run, which I did as fast as I could.

I skimmed across the sand like a startled stallion but stopped in my tracks when two men came running out of the jungle, heading me off. I looked behind me to find the shooter emerging from his hiding place, cutting off my retreat the other way.

I looked to the jungle and contemplated making a run for it, but quickly discarded the idea. It was too dense, and the sword wielding foes before me would have probably cut me down from behind before I even made it there.

I would have to fight again, and as they approached nearer, I recognised it was the same man I had fought back in town with two of his friends. They had followed me, and waited for me to be alone, and now I was at their mercy.

I just hoped I'd make a good account of myself.

'Have you come for another thrashing then?' I said cocksure of myself, trying to make a last show of defiance.

'I think it's going to be you taking a thrashing whippersnapper,' the man holding the smoking musket replied smiling. His dark curly beard had matted with sweat from waiting in the hot foliage of the jungle. He had stayed concealed until the perfect moment to fire upon me.

'Would you at least let me put my clothes on before we begin? I can't very well fight like this.' The men with swords laughed at my attempt at humour. The man, who I had beaten, spat a gob of tobacco in my direction, and sneered at me without mercy.

'There won't be much fighting lad. We're going to cut that little tagger off and feed it to the birds anyway. I'm going to enjoy hearing you scream, just like those damn niggers.'

I was about to launch myself at him but stopped myself when I heard a hiss come out of the jungle and an arrow thump with a sickening thud into the slavers neck.

His eyes went wide, and he dropped the empty musket, holding both ends of the arrow that had torn through his throat, chocking him where he stood.

After a few seconds of incredulous shock, he sank to his knees and killed over, with frothing blood gurgling onto the pale Jamaican sands.

The other two looked into the jungle nervously. They were not quite sure what to do now their leader had been slain by the unseen archer. I however knew exactly who had fired the arrow, and I boldly swept up the fallen musket from the lifeless hand of my downed attacker.

The men fearing for their lives but still bent on murder, charged together hoping to skewer me with their swords. I batted the pair of blades away, using the musket like a club. Another arrow thumped into the flank of one of them, and he fell to his knees and cried out in agony.

The last man standing did not run for his life, to his credit.

Instead he charged up the beach to where the arrows had come from. He had clearly considered that to be the greater threat and darted left and right to spoil the archers aim. He did not stand a chance though, even with his darting and dodging.

The man in the jungle could take out a brace of speeding rabbits on the run with little effort.

So, the man blundering up the beach in temper would be child's play, and easy pickings for the expert marksmen.

Another arrow flew from the treeline, this time hitting him in the leg, and dropping him into a heap. He screamed just as his fellow had, and I advanced on him from behind, to cease that shrill noise.

At the treeline, the archer emerged. His bow was already strung with an arrow, ready to fire.

He nodded at me, grinning at my nakedness. Samuel The Poacher lay down his bow, and pulled a pistol from his leather holster, and walked towards the stricken foe as if he were taking a leisurely stroll.

'You see; the bow will always be better than the gun John,' he shouted to me over the noise of the screaming attacker.

'I never doubted it Sam,' I said, relieved to still be alive.

Samuel had saved me once again, and I was glad I had asked him to join my merry band. He was to me, as little John was to Robin Hood and without him that day I would not be writing this story now.

I wanted to know what he was doing in the jungle but turned when I heard a gun being cocked behind me. 'Look out John!' cried Samuel.

I froze in place, unable to move my body in time before the shot was fired. The second man Sam had hit in the ribs, had crawled over to his leader and relieved him of a pistol, which he then pointed at me. I closed my eyes and grimaced from the certain impact.

But the shot I had heard did not come from the man before me, and I opened my eyes to see him in wonder, with a neat hole, dead centre of his forehead. He fell on top of his leader, killed before his face hit the sand.

'I owe you thanks thrice now Samuel.' I said to my guardian angel.

He lowered his own smoking pistol casually.

'Thrice?' He asked me confused.

'You saved me in the tavern when we arrived here, then you saved me from those two wretches.' I said to him gratefully.

'What about this one?' he asked. 'Don't I take credit for this one too.' he laughed.

'No… I would have taken this one easily,' I jested with no small amount of panic still in me. 'How did you know they would follow me?'

'I saw them leave, all excited down the beach. I knew you'd come for a lone walk and thought you could use a hand. I was right.' I clapped him on the shoulder and wrapped my arms around him in thanks.

'I am glad you're safe John, but I should remind you that you're still not wearing cloths man,' he said in an uncomfortable voice. I let him go, and we walked over to where the last of them still moaned from his wounded leg.

He had snapped off the quivered end of the arrow and tried to pull the stump out with little success. The barbed point held fast, and he shrieked with pain for his efforts. The arrow had taken him in the upper thigh and pulling the shaft had only caused the wound to bleed more profusely.

I could smell the bloods metallic scent, as we stood over him, not quite sure whether to put him out of his misery and make the world a better place for it.

'Well if you're going to do it, just kill me and be damned.' he shouted at us, with tears of frustration falling down his cheeks. He was the one who had whipped the black man to death at the docks when we had arrived at Jamaica. God, it seemed, had finally punished them for their wicked ways.

'It's no more than what you deserve. But we are not murderers like you,' I told him with disdain. Samuel pulled out another pistol he had holstered in his belt and aimed at the wounded slaver.

'I could do it John, if you give me the word. He will only try again,' Samuel added threateningly. I believed he was capable of it, but self-defence or duty was one thing. Shooting an unarmed man was another. I paused as if considering Sam's offer. I wanted to make the cruel swine sweat awhile. It was small revenge for what he did to his slaves.

'No Sam… Leave him here to rot. He won't make it back to town anyway. Not with a wound like that. Come on let's go.'

'As you wish John,' Samuel said and holstered his pistol again. 'Good luck with that leg there matey. I wouldn't put too much weight on it if I was you,' he added sarcastically. The arrow was bedded in so deep and bleeding so heavily, it was unlikely he would be going anywhere. We were far from town, and he could barely drag himself a yard, let alone the long distance back over the unstable sand.

We left him where he fell and heard him shout his threats to our backs as we left. 'Come back you bastards. I'll find where you live... I'll gut ya family like squealing pigs,' he shouted hatefully at us. We stopped and turned. Sam took out an arrow and notched it expertly on the bow he had picked back up.

'Shall I John? It's no bother.' But I shook my head.

'Come on Sam; let's go home,' I breathed wearily, exhausted from my adventures.

'Very well,' he replied. 'But can you do me a favour?'

'Yes of course,' I said.

'Would you put some bloody clothes on for heaven's sake?' he chided and shook his head in dismay.

I look back at that day and tell myself I should have let Samuel end that evil man on that isolated beach. But the Lord works in mysterious ways. If I could go back and do it all over again I would not have hesitated to fill his body with lead and steel. For what he did later would warrant such an act and save me from much heart ache and devastation.

CHAPTER 23

John Pinney came out to see us before we left, to wish us a safe journey home. 'I am dreadfully sorry for my drunken behaviour the other night. I do hope you can forgive me,' he said apologetically to me. 'Don't worry about it. Thank you for the books Mr Pinney.' The lads behind me were struggling to control their mirth as we said goodbye to the sugar merchant. I carried on as if nothing had happened.

'It's the least I could do for my inappropriate behaviour. I trust you will be discreet when you return to London?' he asked, pulling a grimaced expression. Captain Diggin had told me of his persistent lewd behaviour, but it had been harmless enough. I would not damage a man's reputation for such insignificance. No one was harmed, and I liked to make more friends than I did enemies, no matter what their sexual preferences were.

I did not like the fact that he kept slaves, but he was not lying when he told me he treated them well. Philip, his personal slave, had told me just as much earlier that day, when he begged permission for his master to see us off after his inappropriate behaviour. 'He is actually quite good to us sir,' he had said to me meekly. It was a sad state of affair to witness another man, used and owned like cattle.

I had however made another powerful friend in the West Indies and said farewell to him on a warm sunny day without a single cloud in the sky. One day, I hoped to come back and find those poor men of Africa free.

Aside from my smuggling activities, I would make a point of doing all I could back home for their plight. I would point out the harsh treatment of the slaves in both the Caribbean and the Americas.

But before I could do that, I faced the homeward journey.

We made good time on the voyage back, sailing on a strong wind, which pushed our heavily laden ship across the mass of the Atlantic, as swift as a bird on a stiff breeze. It was good to be back at sea, and I breathed in the air of the ocean with a lighter heart.

It was like an elixir to heal my troubled mind. Our destination was set for London, but I could not resist returning to Prussia Cove to see my Marie and our new child first.

I would like to say that our journey home was without adventure, but I had chosen a life that would be full of it and could not complain. Compared to the cold darkness of the mines, it was a decent and profitable way to earn a living. I would not trade it to go back down those shafts for the world.

We were not without our own unique hardships at sea though. It was a dangerous job, with a great risk of drowning or being taken by soldiers and pirates. The trials and close shaves we faced were a daily occurrence, but our rewards for the risks we took were worth it.

That risk found us once again, maybe a week or so from the British shores, where French ships still harassed any merchants or naval vessels, like hounds scenting a fox. The British ships were just as notorious in this activity, making the sea around Europe and the British Isles treacherous for all sailors, of all nationalities.

'What is it James?' I asked my startled partner, whose face had tuned quite pale.

'French ship John; it's not a big one, maybe slightly bigger than us,' he said trying to stay composed.

Captain Diggin took the telescope from him.

I was not in charge of the ship as such. My role on the ship had been as an agent for our employers. James for all his maritime skill, served as first mate, so it would be down to them on what course of action we would take.

Never the less, I was a natural leader, even at a young age, and both men looked to me for guidance. The problem we faced was simple; did we run, or did we fight the French ship that bored down upon us. It was very similar to our near fatal encounter with the last French ship, off the Virginian coast.

The only difference now, was the fact we did not have the luxury of a craggy coast to snare our pursuers on. Nor did we have a storm to aid our deliverance from our foe. The weather was clear, and the sun was shining, and as I gazed through the telescope I observed something on the French cutter that did not seem right.

'Captain Diggin, have a look at those gun ports on the lower decks,' I said, handing the telescope to him to see if he saw the same thing I could. It was an expensive telescope, and I was glad that I had purchased it. Captain Diggin smiled as he saw the same thing that I had seen.

'There are no guns on the lower decks. They've just painted the gun ports red to trick an enemy into thinking they have the mightier vessel,' he said laughing.

I took the telescope back and looked once again at the French cutter that came for us with lethal intention.

'Can we out run her Captain? 'I asked, knowing that we probably could not. We had a full load of sugar on board and would make a fine prize for any naval vessel. 'We can't,' he said simply.

'Very well… let's have a fight and see who can capture who. What say you men?' They all cheered at my boast, and Captain Diggin nodded consent, giving the order to prepare for action.

There was a frenzy of activity, as the crew set to tasks which we had drilled into them to pass the time on the way to Jamaica. Now those drills were paying off.

Our experienced crew of former West India Company men led the less experienced, and in no time, we were coming alongside the French ship with a full complement of cannon, primed to fire.

We approached in utter silence, until the peace was suddenly broken by Captain Diggin.

'Fire!' He screamed at the top of his voice, which carried to the furthest parts of the ship. The booming cannons blasted in unison, reaping the French deck with grape shot. We did not want to sink the enemy you see. We wanted to do the same thing it was trying to do to us; which was to capture it whole.

In retaliation, they fired back at us mere seconds later. I felt the heated wind of shots passing only inches from me.

James had been standing to my right, and the shot took his arm clean off his body and left him sprawling on the deck in pools of his own blood. No scream passed his lips, so sudden was his shock at being hit so ferociously by the hell fire being spat at us from the enemy. Only a few other men went down. Some were screaming for help and their mothers.

Samuel The Poacher fired muskets one after the other as a lad handed him guns which had been preloaded with shot. We were so close to the French ship, I could smell the garlic on their breath.

They had also taken a horrible toll of dead and wounded, more it seemed than we had. Every hammer that fell from Samuel and a few other muskets, found their mark, and another of the enemy crew dropped from sight.

Time seemed to slow down in that moment of flame and fury. Our pass had been a matter of seconds but had felt as if we were pressed together like lovers for an age.

As we passed eventually, Samuel was handed his long bow, which had incredible range, and he went about firing shaft after shaft with lethal accuracy. He aimed for officers and when they fell, the ship found they were leaderless and without direction. With one single pass we had decimated them. They lost the stomach for more death and made a run for it with what little crew they had.

Captain Diggin was impressive to watch, going about his business like a true master of the seas. I had chosen my captain and crew well.

While they set course to follow our enemy in good order, I stood on the deck paralysed, just staring at my partner James and the rest of the fallen. I had seen my fair share of blood before, but the havoc from the short battle had rendered some of my crewmen beyond recognition.

Some lads had half of their faces missing, and poor old James lay against the main mast, pale as a ghost from the blood he had lost.

A doctor used to attend the mine from time to time and treat the wounded when there was a collapse or other accident, which were numerous I might add. I had watched him on one occasion, when a man had lost his hand after a collapsed tunnel. He was brought to the surface and I watched him tie rope around the arm, pressing clean cloth against the wound, stemming the flow of blood dramatically.

I came to my senses and cursed myself for falling into a stupor, rushing to James's side to give him what aid I could. His wounds were terrible, and I ripped his soaked shirt off him, and threw the now red clothing away and looked at his chest to see if any of the grapeshot had hit his torso. Unfortunately, it had.

His chest was pock marked with holes where superheated metal had cut right into his lungs. He coughed blood and tried to speak.

'We've... had a good run eh John... you and me.' He threw his head back in anguish and made a gargling sound, spraying a crimson mist into the air to clear the blood in his mouth.

'You'll be fine man, we'll have more adventures, just you see... Can someone fetch me some rope and cloth!' I shouted, knowing deep down that my futile attempt to save him was useless. I turned back to him, and held my friend tight, trying to control his jerking body. Tears streamed down my cheek, and it took a forcible effort not to sob over him like a baby. He in contrast was the epitome of dignity and composure.

Samuel came with the rope and cloth and slid along the deck on his knees in his haste to save James. 'Hang on James!' he said,

The King of Prussia Cove

while wrapping him with linen, which was soaked through in an instant.

'Goodbye lads,' whispered James, before the life in his eyes glazed over. Like a candle nipped out, he died in my arms.

'Damn them… They will pay for this,' promised Sam, who covered our friends face with the linen he had brought.

I lowered my head in sorrow at the loss and kissed the top of his head before laying him down gently. With my eyes closed, I swore to avenge my friend's death and that of the other crew who had lost their lives to the predators who we now pursued.

'James is dead Captain,' I said as I came alongside Diggin, still emotional from the incident. He shook his head and cursed quietly under his breath. I hated swearing. I had made a rule before we sailed that no one on board could swear, and punishment would be given to those that did. The Captain had shared my dislike for uncouth behaviour, and supported this rule, but even he was compelled to utter an obscenity in the dire situation we were in.

The correct course of action would have been to lick our wounds and withdraw from the engagement. It would be a small victory to sail away with our cargo and our lives. But I, like the men was angry at the French for what they had done; and so, we made all speed in haste to seek our revenge.

'Can we catch them Captain?' I asked.

'No,' he said simply. 'But I won't let them get away without trying… Your First Mate now John!' he added, and spat in the direction of our enemy, who extended the gap between us further and further. They were nearly out of sight before one of the crew spotted another ship approaching our foe on the distant horizon. We all held our nerve, hoping that the French hadn't found an ally, and turn around to finish us off.

We were only a merchant vessel, and even if we were a considerably well-armed merchant vessel, our sluggish craft was still no match for two warships.

'Can you see the flag Sam?' I shouted up to where Samuel had climbed the main mast for a clearer view. I waited for his reply, but we were still a fair distance away from the ship, swooping in front of our pray to either link up, or attack it.

'It's British!' he called down excited. 'Praise God… we have them now men,' Captain Diggin said to the crew.

His face was red and screwed up with tension, as he watched the British ship open with a full broadside of cannon. All shots must have landed harmlessly into the sea. The French however knew they were trapped, and would have to run for it, or fight us both one by one, before we joined forces and slaughtered them.

The British ship fired again, and the high intentional aim knocked over the enemy's mast, making them nigh on dead in the water.

We could see the two vessels come close, and lines were thrown over by the British to secure them together. By the time we reached the conflict, the fighting on deck had turned bloody. The noise of the clash of steel on steel echoed to our ears while we secured The Atlas to its port side. I fired both pistols at two Frenchmen who rushed at us in an attempt to stop us boarding. My two shots hit them in their torsos, and they crumpled to the floor together. The rest of our crew leapt over with swords in hand, and bayoneted muskets, thrusting without mercy. The French came at us, still with numbers enough to repel our small band of boarders before we had gained a foot hold. They hadn't the time to reload their muskets after firing once upon the British on their starboard side. The swine's fought with my lads, gun to gun, in a gruelling battle of wills.

Still on The Atlas, Samuel released more of his lethal arrows, hitting men with every shaft once again. The sword work I had learned back in England, would now be put to good use, and I parried and thrust into the stomach of a large bearded brute. To my right, a bayonet was pocked towards my face, which I instinctively ducked and swung the sharp edge of my heavy cavalry sword in a powerful stroke, cutting the man's leg clean off just below his knee. The noise and screams of the fallen was haunting in a way, but I rejoiced as I noticed that none of my crew were among the fallen. We ploughed into them until we reached the British on the other side of the crowded deck.

The French could see their deaths in our vengeful eyes, and sensibly, they surrendered as one. Our men cheered alongside our new allies, who did not waste any time in securing the prisoners of war.

To my utter astonishment, I recognised the man leading the British attack. He walked over to me smiling and was just as shocked to see a friend in the most unlikely of places.

'John Carter! Is it truly you?' William Vingoe said brightly.

'It is my friend, it is... I can't believe you are here William,' I said incredulously to the man who had given me my start into the world of smuggling. I had come to his father, John Vingoe's aid, and they had given me the opportunity to escape the tin mines forever. I now stood once again before my friend who had joined the British Navy on my behalf, and once again, I was in his debt for his intervention.

'God must have sent you to earth as my guardian angel William,' I said, taking his hand gratefully. 'You must have been mad to try and take this bugger on your own. I heard you were bound for Jamaica,' he replied, grasping my shoulder in firm companionship.

'We're returning home from there with a full cargo of sugar. This cursed ship thought to take us as a prize,' I said in way of explanation. 'How quickly the tables can turn at sea eh... We've been patrolling these waters looking for a fight and some booty,' he said pointing down at the deck.

As we spoke to one another, our men from both ships herded the captured French below decks, and secured them and their vessel, putting a skeleton crew in place to bring her back to Falmouth. William was devastated to learn of James's fate. He was not a religious man like me, but he spoke for the dead men we lost with Captain Diggin, who said some wonderful words for James and the rest of the men who had fell that day. We buried them at sea and returned home together in convey.

Before we boarded our own ships, we looked around on the French vessel, which was named La Belle.

'How goes it in the navy then my friend?' I asked William as we poked around the hold, looking for something valuable. 'I can't complain really. The pay is bad, but the spoils of war we get to keep. It's just as profitable as smuggling or wrecking to tell you the truth.'

He had not been exaggerating or boasting when he said that. His ship The Wolf, had plagued the French, Dutch and Spanish ships along with the rest of the British Navy. With the skills he had learned as a smuggling man, he had become a Captain with a reputation for victories.

We found a locked chest full of money, weapons and ammunition and split everything two ways, making my round-trip voyage most profitable indeed. William had full claim on La Belle, because we had no rights to capture an enemy ship, as we had no letters from the admiralty. That was something I hoped to remedy when I returned home. If things had gone according to plan, then Uriah Tonkin was now Mayor of Penzance and would write a recommendation for me to have the letters of marquee I wanted. I told William that I would do just that, considering how much wealth you could legally acquire from capturing enemy ships.

'I will back you up, and write a recommendation if you like John,' he offered me with an element of sadness in his eyes. He had been cagy with me since his arrival, and I asked him if he was alright.

'Let's sit down and have a drink man,' he said evasively. I was still devastated by the loss of James, and I had assumed he was equally concerned. We sat in his small cabin on The Wolf and he poured some rum for both of us. I told him about our adventurous journey and my plans to trade with Boston merchants once this trip was concluded.

'So, have you got any news from home William?' I asked eager to find out all I could. He looked into his drink and bit his lower lip nervously. 'What is it?' I asked.

'It's Marie John,' he told me uncomfortably. The colour from my cheeks must have drained, and I remember the sick feeling in my stomach at the mention of her name. 'What's happened?'

'She had some difficulties after the birth of your son. Both are alive, and your son is well. But Marie became weak and has been slowly deteriorating. I did what I could when I was there, but her mother was taking good care of her when I left; the baby too.'

I could not take any more sorrow, and stood facing the wall of the small cabin, watching the spiders making their webs on the timber with tears of shame in my eyes. 'I shouldn't have left them,' I admitted.

'You were not to know she would become ill John. All you have done is try to provide a better life for them both. They know that, and she loves you all the more for it.' It was hard to be consoled by him.

I wished at that moment to have been by her side and hold them both in my arms. But I was still a few days away from home frustratingly.

'I should not have left them William,' I repeated, and wiped my eyes. I had so much to do when I returned, that it scared me to my core. I had to see my love and wished beyond hope that she still lived. I had to find the relatives of James and tell them the sad news of his passing. Then I would have to insure my affairs at Prussia Cove were in order. But at that moment, no thought of coin and wealth could brighten my dark mood.

Lastly, I would have to finish my journey, and deliver the cargo of sugar to my employer in London. I promised myself that if Marie was too unwell, then I would send Captain Diggin alone to finish the transaction. William and I embraced in friendship before leaving for our own ships to set course for home. Home at last.

CHAPTER 24

We anchored in Penzance harbour and I presented my legitimate papers to the customs men who did not even bother to inspect my cargo. With Uriah Tonkin as Mayor, inspections had become very few and far between for the right people. Apparently, I was one of those people at last, and was grateful to be left alone to go on my way.

I borrowed a horse in town, and nearly rode the poor creature lame in my attempt to reach my family as quickly as I could. I told the lads to recoup and repair any damage to the ship while I was gone. They would no doubt frequent the many taverns, such as the Turks Head. They deserved a respite after what we had been through together.

After what seemed like an age, I arrived home. There had been many changes at Prussia Cove during my absence. I had left Charles in charge of all activities; including the excavation of the cave system I had wanted to lead up to Bessie's beer house cellar. The cave had been widened, with shelving cut into the rock by some of the best tin minors around. It was Charles who spotted me coming, and he and my other brother Francis, hurried over to welcome me back to my kingdom.

'Praise God John, it is good to see you brother,' Francis said joyfully. He was slightly younger than Charles and had the strong Carter nose and brow like me. The only difference between us was his devotion to the Lord.

As I have mentioned, I have love for our saviour, and still worship as much as possible today. Francis in contrast was feverish about the topic, and would always scorn even me, his oldest brother if he felt that I had sinned.

But it was good to see him never the less. Beyond our differences, our Mother and Father had made us loyal and true to one another.

'It's good to see you both as well, but where's Marie and my son?' I said urgently.

The sweat on my brow, and the frothing foam that had built up around my horse's snout, indicated my haste to get there. 'They are both well at Bessie's place John. Come on, lets introduce you to your son,' Charles said with an enormous smile.

As soon as I heard they were both well, my heart felt instantly lighter, and I felt a pressure inside my head wash away in relief.

I climbed to the top of the cliff with my two brothers and stopped as I noticed a woman hanging out washed garments on a line outside the beer house. The grass was swaying ever so gently in the warm sea breeze, and the sun was starting to set behind my back, casting the women in an angelic glow. There was a wicker basket on the ground with an infant inside, and from my vantage point I could see her talking to the babe, while hanging out the cloths. She had not seen me yet, and I savoured the moment watching them, forgetting that my two brothers where there at my side.

Suddenly she stopped hanging out the clothes, and turned slowly towards me, as if she could sense somehow that I was watching her. Our eyes met between the short distance, and she dropped the cloths and wooden pegs onto the grass, wide eyed, not believing what she was seeing.

I had been gone for just over a year, and she must have thought she was imagining my presence before her. I could see her bosom rise and fall at the sudden sight of me.

I have seen men before fall in love, and never understood why they did such foolish things. Or why they swooned and fussed over each other with no thought of those around them. Finally, I knew how they felt. We were truly in love, and I swore to myself on that tranquil summers evening, that I would never leave her side for so long again.

I ran towards her, and the spell she was under broke, now realising I was real after all. I reached her in moments and we embraced fiercely, without the need to talk to one another. I kissed her, and she kissed back, just as passionately, until eventually I heard the disapproving cough from behind us. Francis would be finding the open display of affection most uncomfortable.

'I'm sorry I've been so long,' I told her with tears in my eyes. She was just as emotional, and I wiped her tears from her cheeks. 'Your back now John; that's all I care about. Your safe and in my arms again,' she said to me smiling now. She turned to the infant, who seemed to be watching the clouds float by happily from his perch inside the basket. 'Your son will be pleased to meet you too.' She took me by the hand towards my baby boy. 'Say hello to your father Thomas.' I laughed at the mention of his name.

'Thomas eh… a fine name for fine young gent. May I Marie?' I asked, meaning to pick him up and hold him for the first time.

'He is your son John; of course, silly.'

I reached down and plucked him from his nest, spinning him around in delight. He had his mother's eyes, as blue as the ocean. He looked me up and down, and opened his mouth happily, enjoying the attention. 'Hello Thomas,' I said.

Marie came up behind me and placed a tender hand on my back. We then held each other as a family for the first time, and it dawned on me that this was the meaning of life. Family is everything. All I was trying to achieve in life, becoming a man of means, becoming more than my father had been, was all for this. I would not let Thomas Carter or Marie have the life of decent poverty as my own farther used to call it.

I would expand my kingdom for them; so, they would have the world if they wished it.

'I've seen William Vingoe recently, while at sea.' I told Marie, as we walked along the Cliffside with Thomas in my arms. 'He told me you were unwell, and I feared you were dying,' I confessed frowning.

'I was near to death after Thomas was born. I had lost a great deal of blood and was in and out of consciousness for weeks.'

'How did you recover your health?' I asked, thanking the Lord for watching over them.

'Lord Arundell heard of my troubles and sent his physician. Thomas was named after him. He saved my life John.'

'Then I owe him everything. I will seek him out and thank him personally. First, I'm afraid I must deliver a cargo of sugar on his friend's behalf. I should be on the waves right now, but I had to see you,' I said taking her hand.

'I'm glad you did. I'm sure Thomas is too.'

'But I have not come home empty handed my dear. I have gifts for both you, and little Thomas. I'll have someone send them to you when I go back,' I said.

'Oh, you can't go yet John, not right away. I won't let you,' she protested, and pulled us both towards her.

'I will stay the night and then go back. Don't worry, I'll not be long. Just a short journey to London, then I'll return and spend some time with you both, I promise.' I wanted nothing more than to stay with them. But I had my principles and would honour any shipment to its conclusion. A man's word is his bond, and I was building a reputation on that principle. When someone wanted me to collect a cargo, or wanted to purchase contraband from me, I would always deliver on time.

Now that I knew my Marie and son were well, I could now proceed to finish the job I had agreed to.

'Very well; we have waited this long I suppose. A while longer won't do much harm,' she agreed reluctantly. 'You must bring me more presents from London though,' she said, and kissed me before I could disagree with her.

During the night we made love for hours, and after that, talked about my adventures abroad. She could not believe the stories of how the Negro men were treated. It had horrified her just as much as it had me. She gasped at the encounters with the French and laughed wickedly about the inappropriate behaviour of Mr Pinney. As the sun rose on the eastern hill, Thomas stirred and opened his eyes, crying for his mother's milk. He had a good appetite like me, and after a full night of activity, I was craving some food also. We had not slept a wink, and Bessie brought us in breakfast, which was scoffed up in moments. Marie looked tired but insisted on showing me the great house I was having built overlooking Prussia Cove, before I left.

The walls of the house were nearly built, and the timbers for the roof were being piled up, ready to be hoisted and fixed. I wanted the house to have commanding views of my cove. I could then observe my shipments, all from the comforts of its luxurious confines. I had taken note of the modern furnishings and styles that the wealthy dressed their houses in. I wanted fine mahogany furniture, and paintings of seascapes and heroes on display.

Above all my hopes and dreams, what I wanted most of all was my own library and study. I knew I could never hope to compete with Lord Arundell's collection of books. But I would build my own collection, and make a small escape for myself where I could read Voltaire, and other great works to become lost in.

Marie walked me into the bare plastered room which would become the library. The lofty heights would be grand indeed. I had insisted on this regardless of expense. For the first time in my short existence, I had disposable income to enjoy a few of the finer things of life. I was nowhere near as wealthy as I am today, or close to the likes of the lords and ladies of Cornwall. But I was doing well for myself, as a young and reputable merchant of goods. Now I was back home, I couldn't wait to expand. We are an enterprising family, and only at the beginning of making serious money and prosperity. While the rich and wealthy heirs of nobles, like Francis Godolphin, squandered their wealth at cards, I reinvested my hard-earned coin to the next venture.

The house I was building would not make me money directly. But indirectly, it acted as a hub for all my business and would be known as Prussia Castle to the cove boys who fished and smuggled around the bay. By the time I returned from London, the house would be weather tight and ready for internal decoration. I would bring most of the furniture and paintings for the house from London, but there was a man locally who could help me stock my library. 'What do you think John? Marie asked excited.

'I love it. It will be a dream comes true. Now all I've got to do, is get the money to pay the builders.'

So off I went to complete my delivery of sugar to London docks. It was hard, as I expected it would be to say goodbye to Marie and little Thomas. She understood that her life of hardship would change dramatically if my fortunes continued to prosper as they were. She wanted the big house just as much as I did, and I was sure she would like the petty coats and dresses I had bought her on my recent travels. I had also purchased an ivory rattle for my new child Thomas. While in the capital I would try to find a decent crib for the little rascal.

CHAPTER 25

The voyage to London seemed to take an age. We skirted around the Kentish coast in The Atlas, and up into the mouth of the Thames river. The multitude of ships and sloops made navigating the estuary quite difficult. We passed the ruin of Hadleigh Castle, which overlooked the Essex side of the river. Years before, in the mid-sixteenth century, the castle was bought by Lord Richard Rich, from Edward VI, for seven hundred pounds. Rich then dismantled it for the value of its stonework, and then passed it to his heirs as a ruin of little value at all. A few houses dotted the hills which slopped down to the river, and we anchored near the Hadleigh ruin, and rowed up one of the many dikes that led towards the old castle. At one time it would have been a crucial fort to observe any enemy fleets coming down the Themes.

We rowed until we spotted life, and then pulled into shore to make enquires of sorts. I still had the sugar to deliver, but I wanted to find out who the local buyers of contraband were. I was always on the lookout for potential deals in those days, and it did not take long to be pointed in the right direction. An old dishevelled looking man told us that there was indeed a man who would be interested in buying and selling contraband.

'His name is Blyth sir, William Blyth of Paglesham,' he said in a thick country accent. It turned out that Paglesham was a hive for smugglers, due to its perfect position on the river Roach.

Just north of the village was the river Crouch, and both rivers met at Foulness Island, were smugglers could float up river and into the many creeks on their flat bottomed luggers. They would unload fish, oysters, but predominantly duty free contraband inland. The customs officers could do very little to stop them because of its isolated position. Just like Prussia Cove, this was the hub and capital of smugglers in the south east of England, and I meant to parley with its ruler and king of smugglers in the county of Essex; Mr William Blyth.

I had taken with us, stores of gin, claret and tobacco from the Cove. A smuggling man must always make good use of any opportunity presented, and it would have been foolish if I had not tried to do business wherever I sailed or travelled to.

We sailed The Atlas as far as we dared up the tidal river Roach, and then rowed the rest of the way upriver with a few parcels of tobacco and claret to show Mr Blyth, if we were so fortunate to find him.

It turned out Blyth was an easy man to find. He was the church warden and the grocer, who sometimes wrapped his goods in pages torn out of the parish record books. Or so I was told.

I found him playing cricket with two of his fellows. It was midday, and I approached the small group lightly armed, with a holstered pistol in my belt, and a cavalry sword sheathed by my side. They stopped playing and turned when they saw me, and ran to where their weapons lay, not far from the cricket stumps. They cocked pistols and were ready for any violence. They were well prepared for ambushes from the customs men no doubt, and I admired them for their diligence.

I raised my hands to let them know I came peacefully and wished to talk. No one raised a pistol at me, but they did not put them away either. 'Good day to you gentlemen,' I said merrily, as if I was just taking a stroll through their village green. 'I'm John Carter.' I introduced myself grandly, taking my hat off and bowed, as if addressing King George himself.

'So?' the leader of the three men said coldly. He was young, maybe in his early twenties, and had a hard, weather-beaten face of a seaman. He wore no shirt and his tanned and muscular body gleamed in the summer sun. His powerful and tall build made him tower over the two other men at his side and I had to choose my words carefully, so as not to cause a misunderstanding.

'I am a Cornish man sir, and deal in certain goods free of duty owed. I understand you and I have the same occupation in common. I am bound for London but could not resist meeting the king of smugglers in the east, and dare I say make a deal or two.' I have always been a charismatic and likable sort of fellow, but I could see the Essex man's suspicion in his eyes.

'How do I know you're not one the excise men from Maldon sir? You could be setting me up for all I know,' he said cautiously.

'I can understand your dilemma sir, but I give you my word I am not. I have a small quantity of goods to barter if you wish to buy. I will give you reasonable prices for what I have to sell,' I said to the still unconvinced Blyth.

'What makes me so special, that you'd come all the way from Cornwall to sell me contraband. Haven't you got men down there to sell your wares to?' he replied, stroking the butt of his pistol with his thumb.

'Oh, I do sir. I have customers aplenty, but you can never have too many you see. I am on my way to London to deliver a cargo of sugar; all legitimate and taxable I might add. But while I was in the area, I thought to seek out a fellow smuggling man and do some good business. I'll take you to my ship if you wish; we are anchored down river from Foulness Island,' I offered, to ease his worries. Apparently, even in the isolated parish, the excise men plagued the smugglers at every turn; more so than we experienced in Cornwall. I could understand his reluctance to do business with a stranger. That was one of the reasons I had come alone to see him.

'I would like to see your ship sir if you wouldn't mind. If what you say is true, then we can do business.'

I did not want to waste any more time than I had to, and rowed them to The Atlas, where I spoke to them of home and of my adventures. Once we got chatting they became mightily friendly indeed and invited me to come back to their local Inn called the Punch Bowel.

It was busy inside, and the people greeted them warmly when they entered. It was like their version of Bessie's place back at the cove, and they ran all their contraband through it.

'Sorry we gave you such a frosty reception Mr Carter. You can't be too carful these days. The excise men would like nothing more than my ruin. I pay most of them off, yet still they endlessly persist to catch us in the act,' Blyth said, and offered me some gin. He was known in town as Hard Apple, because of selling groceries and being a general hard man, and hero of the village.

I let him fill my cup, and we drank late into the night, trading stories and righting the world as we saw fit. We were getting on famously, so I took the opportunity to discuss prices for what I could sell him.

He was a fiend when it came to negotiating. I always prided myself at making good deals, but William Blyth was the canniest man I had ever encountered. In truth, we both enjoyed the bartering, like two chess masters facing off to see who could crown themselves champion.

'Your prices are too high Mr Carter. How am I to make a profit if you will not budge from your position?' he piped up in feigned exasperation.

'The price is not as cheap as the rubbish you're used to. But I can promise you quality goods, and I can supply them in any quantity you wish,' I countered smiling. He wanted what I had to sell, that was plain and simple. But he wanted me to sell it to him at an extortionately low price. His tactic was to just bombard me with figures and persist until I gave in. I however would not be so easily conquered.

'I will make you a compromise sir,' I said in way of showing reason. 'I will sell you my goods, ten percent less than I am asking. If you can distribute it quickly enough and purchase frequently. Then I can keep it at that price,' I offered, knowing I had made a fair deal.

He raised his eyebrows to suggest he was thinking about it. But if he was as big as he said he was, I knew he would accept it.

'Very well Mr Carter, you have a deal,' he conceded finally. We shook on it, and I was pleased that I had gained another foothold so near to my countries capitol. The quantities I was bringing into Cornwall were becoming too large for even my most tenacious of distributors. If I was to expand, then I would have to supply all of the major towns and cities with duty free contraband. But If I had just started selling to the locals without coming to Hard Apple first, then a confrontation would have been certain. But because I had given him a slice of the pie, he would welcome my goods, and potentially become my best and most profitable partner.

Before I left Penzance, I met with my patron John Tonkin and told him of the arrangements I had made in Boston, America.

I had rented a warehouse there and employed an agent to stock the place with cotton and tobacco. I would send back Captain Diggin with a cargo of French claret, gin and brandy, and so keep the route going like that indefinitely. I would sell the cotton in England, and pay the duty owed, making my activities and name appear honourable.

John Tonkin would be pleased when I told him I had now gained access and permission to distribution into London and Essex. His and my prosperity would rise beyond our wildest dreams, as long as we did not make any mistakes, or fall foul to any acts of violence, such as my old partner James, who I had forced to the back of mind in my grief.

CHAPTER 26

We made the trade in London without any problems whatsoever. I didn't meet William Beckford our employer, and I was glad of it. He was a slaver, and owner of many plantations where they inflicted cruelty on a daily basis. I could not say honestly that I could have held my tongue at the barbarity I witnessed. Instead of coming himself, he sent his agent, who expressed gratitude on his behalf. The precious sugar released much needed cash flow to the purse of the Member of Parliament. He paid for his goods and asked if we would transport a number of African slaves to Jamaica and bring back sugar on a permanent basis. This was known as the triangular trading system, were merchants looped around the Atlantic for total profit. Guns or spirits would be taken to Africa completing the process.

I declined out of hand, trying to keep the disgust from my face. I would consider making another sugar run, but the thought of transporting human cargo went against every fibre of my being.

Before going to London, I had thought to explore the metropolis with some of the crew. I had heard the city was no place for a man of the country to linger in. In truth, the place was horrible. The stench was the worst thing of all. I had never smelled anything like it in my life. People threw their raw sewage out onto the very streets and waited for the night soil men to come and clear it away. Cesspools of the waste, lined the roads in sludge and filth, making a mess of any pedestrian, when any horse and coach came along.

The unsavoury aroma was fouled further still by the multitudes of coal fires, which burned within the thousands of homes, causing a smog to oppress the city in a dull cloud of misery. The drinking water available from the Themes was a murky brown and looked so unpalatable; gin stalls were the only way to quench a thirst. Subsequently, most people, especially in the slum areas were normally blind drunk.

After the great Fire of London in 1666, the city had been rebuilt in such haste, and with such poor materials, it was not uncommon for buildings to collapse right on top of you. I walked along the narrow alleyways and feared for my life under the rickety structures. I thought at any moment the cracked brick walls would give way and bring one of the leaning buildings crashing on top of me.

Dead rats, dogs and even the odd horse festered and rotted were they had died in the street. Dieses was rife, and the life expectancy of a poor man of London was little better than working down a mine. It was safe to say that I hated the place, and I could not wait to return to the fresh clean air of my beloved Cornwall. But before I could do that, I had to meet another gentlemen and friend of John Tonkin who lived near the newly built British Museum.

His name was Benjamin Tuddenham, a merchant of tea, who sold his goods to the many tea houses within the city. Tax imposed on tea at the time was over one hundred percent its value, making it the tipple of only the very wealthy. In Cornwall however, most families had pots of tea among other exotic luxuries, which were supplied to them by the numerous smuggling men.

Tea came mainly from Asia, and when a vessel skirted into the English Channel, it would always draw near to the regular spots, were a smuggler could buy some of its cargo, cutting out the revenue owed. Back at Prussia Cove, I had a permanent group of lads, called the Cove Boys, who would row out and trade with the cargo ships. My brother Charles, was leading the lads there, and he could barter just well as any Carter could. The only trouble with Charles was the fact that he did not have his sea legs, and greatly preferred being based on land. It suited me, for I needed someone I could trust to run things there. We had a large store of tea in the cave at the cove and in the crypts of several local churches. Just like in the Essex village of Paglesham, the whole community were involved. The extra income insured they were able to eat and enjoy some comfort in their hard lives.

Mr Tuddenham greeted me into his home, and I was grateful to be off of the packed streets. 'Welcome Mr Carter, I've been expecting you,' he greeted me warmly. 'Would you care for a drink man? I had my own flask of brandy, but I agreed out of politeness.

'Indeed, I would Mr Tuddenham.'

'Call me Ben lad.'

'Only if you call me John,' I replied to the most agreeable merchant. He fetched drinks and then we talked.

'I have a problem John, and our mutual friend tells me you might be the man to help me,' he said in a hushed voice, as if the walls had ears to hear our conversation. He was middle aged and lived a comfortable life. He clearly liked to drink, for his glass was seldom empty while I was there.

'I'm sure I can sir. How can I help?' I asked pleasantly. He stood and broke wind unexpectedly, making the inside of his house stink as badly as it did outside. 'Oh, excuse me. It's the bowels you see. I've been told to eat less meat, but what do they know eh… bloody quacks,' he said, sitting once more and leaned closer towards me. His breath was no better than his backside, and I sat back in the chair and tried not to breathe through my nose.

'You can help me, by selling me some tea. Not at the prices we're charged at the docks mind. If you know what I mean lad?' He laughed as if he had said the funniest thing in the world. I laughed with him, and apart from his bowel movements, I actually found the man entertaining.

'I do know what you mean Ben. I can supply as much tea as you please,' I said to him boldly.

'Well, I can sell a great deal of the stuff lad,' he said seriously, now trying to let me realise the reality of his problem. Just like the shortage of many goods, times were hard for merchants, due to the slow shipping because of the war. When ships did get through and many did, then the prices were exorbitant and difficult to sell to the public who were also feeling the pinch on their finances.

'Then I am your man sir. I can arrange regular shipment to you via the Essex river ways.' I was glad that I had secured a relationship with William Blyth. I would cut him in on the deal of course. I would lose profit by doing that. But it was his territory, and if I wanted to continue to operate and prosper in the east of England, then I needed his involvement. He would be grateful of the business too.

'Splendid, let me introduce you to my man Timothy, he will arrange the collection of goods for me. You can fill him in on the details,' he said and led me to the basement of his home were Timothy was shovelling coal into buckets to be taken around the house. He was a kind and agreeable fellow, and the three of us went over the times and locations of delivery.

The bartering for the price of the tea was nothing like my encounter with Blyth. Ben Tuddenham, agreed to my first proposal, which was high where I came from. Here in the city though, it was cheaper than anything he could get his hands on.

We left London the next day, and I was glad for it, and watched the cloud of smog in the distance as we sailed on our merry way. We passed the ruin of Hadleigh Castle once again, and then headed out to the open sea.

Captian Diggin, along with The Atlas's crew, all agreed to carry out runs back and forth to Boston on my behalf. He and his crew were good at what they did, and I was confident that they would make me and themselves money.

After spending so long with the lads on the ship it was a hard thing to leave them. But I had my family to go home to, and I would see them all again when they returned. I had purchased an immensely comfortable arm chair in London and it would become my throne inside the new house.

When I eventually arrived back at the cove, the slate roof tiles were being nailed to the rafters. The house would be habitable in a matter of weeks. Marie could hardly contain herself at the thought of living in a place so grand. She would have to share the house with members of my family who worked for me at the cove, but that did not matter in the slightest to her. I had a wall built around a quaint little garden, so we could grow flowers, and sit outside on the long summer evenings and watch the sea together.

Eventually the tunnel being dug had lengthened. The natural slipway of the cove would make bringing in goods easy, and the tunnel came out right under Bessie's basement, so we never needed to bring cargo up by land if we did not want to. I had asked the local blacksmith to make us tracks for carts, which we wheeled up to the top of the tunnel on a pulley system. The beauty of the position of Prussia Cove, was the fact that a ship at anchor could not be seen unless you looked directly over the cliff face. My new house was positioned so I could observe the comings and goings in comfort. But it was also a distinct advantage if any customs riders came sniffing around.

The big house was a statement of my wealth and prosperity. It was also rubbing every poor man's nose in the fact that I was faring far better than they were. Francis would often come and chastise me for my greed and sinful behaviour.

'Surly you have enough money to go legitimate John,' he said bitterly one day. 'You could even give a portion to the church,' he added.

'I give the church plenty Francis. Or perhaps you don't see the coin I pour onto the collection plates each Sunday,' I replied annoyed at being told what to do with the money I had earned through blood sweat and tears.

'Yes. But you could do so much more than that. Why carry on living this sinful life when you could follow a much nobler path?'

He was so much like our father. Cautious, and so ready to let others make fortunes from the sweat of his brow. He was coming to the cove a great deal to preach to me about right and wrong. The conversation would always turn to the inevitable; money for the church.

Don't get me wrong; I agree that a man should pay what he could to the Methodist movement. But I was not a man born into the gentry. I had, at a young age, built trading routes with the French. I had acquired warehouses and trade to and from the American Continent, as well as the south east of England. I now owned the farm I was brought up on, and I owned the land around Prussia Cove, where my lads traded with ships from all nations of the world. I was not going to give up money so easily, and end up poor once again, just to satisfy my little brother.

He would always go off frustrated and angry at my refusal to go legitimate. Which may have been my undoing, had I not had word of his foolishness.

I was sipping tea in my new garden when one of the lads from town, barged through my gate in a rush to give his news.

Apparently, my brother Francis had preached in Germoe about me, his sinful brother who was sitting on a fortune from buying and selling contraband. I honestly did not see the act as sinful. The God fearing rich were doing it. If it was a sin to feed one's family without harming another man in the process, then I would face that judgment with open arms when the time comes. It was strange that my brother could see no wrong in the enslavement of the men of Africa, explaining that it was Gods will that they serve their white owners. But he had a big problem with smuggling and all it stood for.

'Your brothers causing a right fuss John,' said the lad who worked on a nearby farm. Thankfully, he also distributed for me on the side.

'There were customs men listening to him and everything. They're on their way here now,' the boy said, breathing hard from his long run to warn me. 'Are you sure they're coming?' I asked, standing from my rest in the garden. He nodded and sucked in more air to catch his breath.

'Francis! What have you done you fool?' I said to the sky, angry at how stupid he had been to place our lives in jeopardy. I ran, and once again had to hide the large amount stored in the caves below. It was not the only cave we used to house our cargoes. We had caves all along the coast from here to Porthleven. The duty men however were coming to my home to search for contraband, which would potentially see me once again in front of a magistrate.

We moved as much as we could into the abandoned mine, using the hidden shaft to hide most of the goods which we could not explain away. But there was too large a quantity to hide it all.

Eventually five riders on horseback came to my house.

I had not seen the men before, and was glad Arthur, The Ferret, Ferris was not with them. The leader of the riders dismounted and walked over to the house expressionless and entered through the front door without invitation. The house was clear of anything incriminating, as was Bessie's beer house. But if he searched the cove below, then I would be finished; all because of the big mouth of my brother.

'Where is it Carter? Save me the trouble of crawling around in the dirt and ruining my uniform eh,' the young customs rider announced, looking pleased at his own remark. I could have tried to fight them off my land, but I was well aware that to harm a customs man in the course of carrying out his duties was a hanging offence. Instead I tried a different tact; one that had worked for me before.

'I am at a loss sir. You seem to know who I am…'

'My name is Davis,' he said, cutting me off abruptly. 'You are correct; I do know who you are. Arthur Ferris has told me all about the upstart from the Godolphin mine. You're also correct in saying that you're at a loss. Your own brother has told us you have contraband here. So where is it Carter?'

Upstairs, Thomas was crying loudly. Marie must have been scared at the presence of the duty men, but all I felt was calm.

Davis was picking up a silver trinket and sniffed it for reasons I knew not. They would find cases of French brandy in the caves below if they found the entrance. I could easily have claimed that I had found it as salvage for the Arundell's, just as I did the last time to get off the hook. But I sensed something about Mr Davis. I believed I had a God given talent for reading peoples characters.

I had sensed the opportunity to bribe Lieutenant Domenici when I was his prisoner in France. Davis for reasons I could not explain gave me that same feeling. Like a dog scenting a bitch on heat, I acted out of instinct.

'Do they pay you well Mr Davis?' I asked with mock curiously, knowing they did not pay them well at all. 'Are you offering me a bribe sir?' he asked me wide eyed. I had committed myself and continued unfazed by his supposed outrage at my question.

'I am not sir. I am however offering you a job and regular income for you and your men out there. You of course will receive the greater sum. I will pay you monthly, and all I require in return is your discretion and information.' I let the silence hang as he weighed up what I had offered him. He stared at me with hard eyes, and for a moment I felt I had misjudged the situation.

'If I turn you in; I will have reward enough Carter. Besides, I doubt if you can afford my discretion,' he said coldly.

'Well let me see; in theory sir, you have not found anything to incriminate me. Even if you did; I would challenge you to find a jury to vote against me. You know as well as I do how things work. My only wish is to compensate a good British citizen with a wage he deserves. For a man such as you are, I think I could stretch to a monthly payment of... one pound per month; half of that a month for your men outside.'

His stubborn face softened instantly. He had expected a few brass farthings for his troubles. What I had offered was more than he would earn as a customs rider. In that moment, I had him.

'You could afford to pay me and the lads that much?' he asked incredulously.

I could have paid him more if he had pushed it. Someone as valuable as a customs rider on my side was worth his weight in gold. But like any deal I made, my first offer was my lowest. He might have worked for me for less, but the amount I offered would be too much for the lowly paid rider to refuse.

'Yes. I can pay you that Mr Davis. If you give me good information and assist me further, I can compensate you handsomely. Just think how happy your wife will be with the extra income you bring to the table. You do have a wife, don't you?'

'I do,' he answered cheerfully. I could see him adding up the sums of money I would pay him in his head. I was considered an exceptional young man by local folk. There were men as young as I was then, with means enough to live the life I was leading. But they on the most part came from wealthy families. The likes of myself and the Vingoe's had earned our place in the world. We were not satisfied with the crumbs that a working wage paid. Instead, we created our own wealth by providing goods in high demand. It was not an easy profession, but now I had money to spend, I realised how easily a man could be tempted by its power.

I pulled out my purse, knowing there was about six pounds inside, and threw it to him. He plucked it out of the air and weighed the purses contents by rocking his hand up and down.

'Call that an advance payment sir.' He opened the bag to inspect its contents, still not quite believing his turn of fortune. 'Do we have an agreement Mr Davis?' I added, smiling and offering my hand to seal the deal. He took it and the deal was done.

'There is nothing of concern here Mr Carter. Thank you for your hospitality.'

'You are most welcome. In a month's time, and every month after that, I will have a lad bring you some coin; as token of my appreciation for all the good work you do for King and County of course.'

'Of course,' he agreed.

'I will also send you word and honour my end of the bargain Mr Carter. Good day to you and your wife.' He nodded to Marie who had been standing behind me, holding the now docile Thomas. When he left with his men, she looked visibly flushed by the incident.

The King of Prussia Cove

'I would've never have believed it if I had not seen it with my own eyes,' she said impressed at what she had just witnessed.

'Just another day's work my dear,' I replied casually. She had heard me tell her stories about negotiating with men in my world. But it had been the first time she had ever seen me do it. I had bargained with the brewess, her mother, but I had always given into her terms easily. It must have impressed her, as later; we lay the sleeping Thomas in his crib and made love like we had never done before.

Afterwards I considered letting her see me work more often, if it caused her to be that affectionate.

I called outside for the young lad who had brought the message of warning and told him to come into the house. I gave him a pound for his efforts. 'I want you to take a message for me young man,' I told him, now fuming from the cause of the betrayal. 'Yes Mr Carter,' he said dutifully.

'Take a message to my brother Francis for me.' I was becoming red in the face from my anger.

'What shall I tell him sir?' he asked, as I looked outside the window brooding.

'Tell him not to come to the cove again. He may return to the farm if he wishes, but I don't want to see him there if ever I come to visit. Have you got that?' He nodded eagerly. 'Good; then go tell him lad.'

CHAPTER 27

Over the next few years a steady stream poured in from my many supply routes, yielding me and my family a great deal of money. Lord Arundell always got his share, and for my loyalty he let me operate unhindered, and helped me to gain my Letters of Marque from the Admiralty. John Tonkin had already been a rich man, long before he made my acquaintance. Since our partnership he had virtually quadrupled his fortune. He was the youngest son from a wealthy family, and although he had been given the means to help himself; he still had to go out in the world alone. He like me, was prospering far beyond his expectation. He was an agent of Lord Arundell, and so he was expected to do his dirty work sometimes. Especially whenever there was a feud between them, and families such as the Borlace's. This meant that he was expected to run for Mayor when Uriah Tonkin stepped down from the contest.

  With the connections we had, it was a foregone conclusion when he was elected Mayor of Penzance. Smuggling as a consequence became so easy, that we could have unloaded our cargos right in front of the duty men at the docks, without so much as a slap on the wrist. Paying Mr Davis turned out to be a very good move on my part. He was an intelligent and capable man. He was catching just enough smugglers to earn promotion, which was good for me. The higher he climbed, the more influence he would gain. I even raised his payments when he was promoted, to encourage his rise further.

Once I got to know him, I decided that I liked him. All he wanted to do was do well by his family. He was not like the bully boys who joined up, so they could push people around, like Arthur The Ferret Ferris. Our arrangement was in the ignorance of all save my closest partners. If Ferris found out he was being bribed, then it would not surprise me if he tried to have Davis hanged.

John Tonkin was told that we had a man on the inside among the duty men. He thought the move was a good one too; so good in fact that he offered to put up the money for half of their monthly payment. He would make good use of that arrangement, as did I.

We enjoyed a golden era, where coin flowed into our pockets like an endless spring. My cousin Henry was bringing in French brandy and claret from our contact, Lieutenant Domenici in France, and paying for it all with Cornish wool. We had regular ships going back and forth to my warehouses in Boston. The outbound cargo would be spirits and wine, and we would bring back cotton and tobacco, which we smuggled both ways.

The British had nigh on destroyed the French fleet by then, and shipping transatlantic cargoes consequently became far less treacherous. We had our accidents of course, especially around the violent seas of the Cornish coastline. Some of our sloops crashed against the rocks killing everyone on board. Thankfully those disasters were rare. We always gave the families of those lost a tidy sum to help them in their dark hour of need.

My greatest skill and natural talent has always been in dealing with people. Because of this talent, I had an enormous number of customers to buy my contraband, and loyal lads to distribute the large amounts of cargo coming in on a weekly basis. The Cove Boys, when they were not stopping merchant ships to trade with, caught fish, which we then sold in Helston, Marazion and Penzance. I would have no time wasted, idling the days away while we waited for shipments to arrive.

Around the Land's End peninsular my partnership with the Vingoe family was flourishing.

John Vingoe, William's father, had introduced me to the world of smuggling, and I felt that I owed him for that; even though I had helped them fight off Irish pirates. They had given me the start I wanted.

He and his family were getting regular shipments from me and traded with folks from there to the Mumbles in Wales.

I had not looked back since that beginning they gave me. I hoped my father could see how successful I was becoming and approve at least on the fact that the Carter family were well cared for. I did not hate him for going down the mine. It was an honest job for honest pay. But I could never let another man break me slowly like that. Most of the miner's worked themselves into early graves, as did he; no better than the slaves of Africa.

As I stood on the Cliffside at Prussia Cove, on one glorious spring day, I realised that I had achieved my dreams before I had even turned thirty. Behind me, Marie was chasing Thomas through the wild flowers and grasses. My mother had come to stay with us at the big house, and she walked along the coastline not far from me with my second child, who I had named Elizabeth after her grandmother Bessie. She was a spirited girl, and already had thick curls of brown hair. Mother was singing to her and picking some flowers for the house which she collected in a basket.

The house was now long finished, and I had asked my mother to come and stay with us. She refused as I expected she would. Her home was on the farm, and she did not want to give up her independence. I was so like her in that regard.

She did not stop my brothers and sisters coming to the cove to work and live though. The farm after all was not far to travel to. Breage was only an hour or so away on horseback, and most of my siblings came and went as they pleased.

The cove had become a busy place, and I loved it. People, I had learned, were the real happiness of life. Money made a person comfortable, and to an extent free. But people were what made life worth living.

My mother made her way to me to where I sat looking out to sea. She brought my daughter Elizabeth with her, who was wriggling in her arms mischievously. I would often come outside and watch the waves.

'Your daughter needs a change I think John,' she informed me, screwing her face up at the prospect of yet another nappy change.

'I could ask Marie to do it Mother?' I said helpfully. I would not dare to lend a hand in that regard.

'Oh, that's alright, I don't mind,' she volunteered, and went about changing Elizabeth who kicked and gurgled, disinterested. 'I wanted to talk to you actually John.'

'What is it?' I asked, knowing where she was leading the conversation. 'It's about your brother Francis.'

'No mother… I don't wish to discuss him,' I said stubbornly.

'He is your brother John, your blood,' she reasoned in her usual way. 'That did not stop him from betraying me. Family doesn't do that to each other. If it had been Arthur Ferris, then I would have been taken to the nearest gallows. All because I would not stop what I do,' I replied, trying to stay calm before my mother, who would still clip me round the ear no matter how old I was.

'He is your brother,' she repeated softly, like I had not even spoken. I thought about what she was telling me and decided he could never be involved at the cove. 'He will not come here mother. It's too dangerous. Men know what he did, and they will not treat him well for it,' I said.

'He doesn't want to come here. He wants to go off and follow John Wesley around Cornwall and save souls. But he does want your forgiveness. I want you to forgive him.' She was becoming emotional at the rift between two of her kin. I rarely witnessed my mother becoming sad like that. Even in the days when we had it hard, and my father used to come home and scream at us all. She would always wink at me, showing a brave face. But it was tearing her up that her sons had become enemies. I would have to make a compromise.

'Tell him I forgive him. I will never forget what he did. But I will not turn from him any longer,' I agreed at last. 'He still should not come here though,' I added. 'I understand; thank you John,' she said, and squeezed my arm affectionately the way all mothers do and walked baby Elizabeth back into the house.

'Everything alright John?' Marie called out form where she played with Thomas.

'Family!' I called back in way of explanation. 'You can't live with them, and you can't live without them.'

CHAPTER 28

'You have been invited to a Ball sir,' John Tonkin told me across the table. I stopped eating the beef and ale pie I was devouring and looked up at his jest. 'A Ball?' I laughed. 'Am I to be the entertainment?' The rain beat against the smeary windows of the Admiral Benbow in Penzance where we ate together. John Tonkin was in fact not joking about the invitation at all. 'Here,' he said, sliding the fine paper towards me. It was the sort of paper that only the rich used. It was wax sealed with the crest of the Arundell's upon it. I broke the wax and read the beautifully penned words of invitation to the Arundell's annual Ball. I had known the family for many years by then, but never would I have dreamed of attending, or being asked to a gathering of the gentry. I could understand his reluctance in the past. Why would he have asked a poorly dressed son of a miner? I would have stood out like a sore thumb years ago.

But now I was becoming a man of means, and the clothes I wore reflected my new position of respect in society.

Lord and Lady Arundell would never see me as their equals, but times were changing. Wealthy merchants were climbing the social ladder, and I could call myself one of them. They would see me as one of their prodigies. I had no doubt that they wished to show me off to their friends, like some accomplishment they had created. I could not care less if they wanted to parade me at the Ball. I owed them that much for the favour they had showed me. I was also thinking of the opportunity of the occasion for my own benefit.

There would be Lords and Ladys, Merchants and Land owners in attendance. Like any wedding, it would be a fabulous place to do business with people, all in one day. If I was given the right introductions, then the Ball could launch me even further on my quest to greatness.

'Well,' I said with my eyebrows raised for the honour. 'I had best go buy some new cloths.' John Tonkin clapped me on the shoulder, pleased for me. 'Well done man. You deserve it. Don't worry about a thing, I will steer you in the right direction. You do know how to dance don't you?' he asked encouragingly. I swallowed nervously because I did not know how to dance. Neither did Marie.

He could see my discomfort and rolled his eyes at me. 'Fear not Carter; I will send the wife over, to show you the basics.'

He was true to his word, and his wife and he came to our house, where we danced and waltzed around the wild flowers of the garden. Marie was horrified when I told her we had been invited to the Arundell's Ball.

'I will be a laughing stock John,' she told me in tears. 'They will think I am the help, and ask me to fetch them refreshments,' she protested miserably. 'They will not Marie. Gentry or not, if you are insulted or ridiculed in any way, then they will feel my boot on their noble backsides, you mark my words,' I said to reassure her unsuccessfully. In the end it had taken a shopping trip in the market town of Helston, where I had the dress maker transform my beloved into a princess, worthy of any Ball in the entire world.

She wore a high white wig that had cost more than I would like to mention. It was worth it though, to see the look on her face as she twirled around in a yellow silk dress she wore. She was enchanting, and the reflection in the dressmaker's mirror before her also took her own breath away. She never knew how beautiful she was until that moment, and I think at last she felt she could walk among the rich and wealthy with her head held high.

I was also spanking in my new attire. I wore a dark blue jacket and trousers, and had polished leather shoes which I could almost see my own reflection in. John Tonkin helped me choose a wig and lent me a cane with a solid silver handle.

Fully dressed in our garden at the cove, we had lads play a fiddle and flute, as we improved our dancing ability under the strict tutelage of Isabelle Tonkin, John's wife. She did not let us rest until we had mastered the moves for each song. Like my instruction for using a sword from William Vingoe, or Samuel The Poacher teaching me how to shoot a gun and bow, I picked up dancing relatively easily. So too did Marie. Isabelle Tonkin was an excellent instructor, and after a long day of stepping on each other's toes, Marie and I became proficient enough to hold our own.

***

The Ball itself was everything and more I had imagined it would be. We arrived together with the Tonkin's and made our way along the multitude of lanterns that lit the way down the neat gravel path leading to the Arundell home. Its great doors were already open, and two wigged servants bowed to us as we entered.

Once inside we were each given glasses of wine, which no doubt came from a smuggled supply I had sold to the Arundell family. They were of course one of my biggest investors, but paradoxically were also my best customers.

John Tonkin introduced me to land owners and merchants, while Marie was taken by the arm by Isabelle Tonkin, and taken to a nearby group of young ladies. I glanced over to them occasionally to check on her but should not have worried. She had her mother's talent for conversation and all of the ladies that gathered around her were clearly enjoying her company. There was only one small group inside the ballroom that looked over at me and Marie with visible distaste on their faces.

The Godolphin's had heard of my swift rise and would always mock me and my family whenever they came to the local taverns, to rub shoulders with the riff raff under their employment. I had not doubted those stories, nor had I cared. On that night however, I tried to avoid them like the plague.

'Ah… Mr Carter, I am so glad you have come. Watch out for Lady Arundell mind, she will want to hear about one of your adventures no doubt,' Lord Arundell said, welcoming me to his Ball. 'It's always a pleasure to entertain her ladyship my lord. Thank you for the honour of inviting me.' I replied grateful.

'The pleasure is all mine.' He took me by the arm and led me over to where some gents sipped claret. They had heard of me through reputation and Lady Arundell who spotted me, joined the group and made the introductions on here husbands behalf.

'This is John Carter, who I have been telling you all about. Do tell us about your trip to the West Indies,' she pleaded with me.

I told them of my battles with the French and nearly losing my life on both occasions. I told them of the profits to be made from smuggling goods into the American colonies. Then I was asked about the slaves I had seen, and I could not help but preach about my true feelings on the matter. Thankfully most of them seemed just as horrified at the hideous treatment of the African slaves. When I described the poor Negro man I had witnessed being whipped to death, Lady Arundell gasped, and covered her mouth with her hand at my bloody tales.

Soon her ladyship left to converse with her other guest's and matters in the group I was with turned to business. They wanted to know the ins and outs of smuggling, and I looked to Lord Arundell like a child seeking approval. He nodded his consent discreetly, to indicate that the men were trustworthy.

'I hear that you are making people a great deal of money Mr Carter. And that is despite the obvious difficulties with the war on,' a man in the group said to me.

'Times of war can be most profitable indeed,' I agreed.

'Actually, I would be extremely interested in purchasing a great deal of tea and claret from you sir, brandy too if you have it.'

The man was a land owner from Gloucestershire who could distribute a great deal of the contraband I was bringing in. The noble men present in the group, put great risk upon themselves by dealing with the likes of a smuggler like me. But the rewards for their troubles far outweighed that risk. I agreed terms with many a gentleman that night. Some who wished to buy goods from me, and some who wanted to finance more voyages, which gave me an enormous line of credit to grow and prosper. It was not surprising that I had found such accommodating gentlemen that night. They could see that I was good at what I did. Naturally they would want the opportunity to profit from me.

Unfortunately, I had become carried away, and in a moment of indiscretion, I boasted that I had a cargo of tea, cunningly concealed on one of my sloops at Porthleven. Francis Godolphin had been standing right behind me while I talked. I had not known how long he had been there, and I tactfully turned the conversation to politics.

'Oh, I wouldn't listen to a criminal's opinion if I was you sir,' Godolphin said, joining us when he realised I had spotted him.

'I beg your pardon sir?' I said stiffly at his rude remark. I had assumed that people acted civilly at Ball's. It appeared I had been mistaken.

'I was just trying to warn this man, not to trust a dirty miner's son, turned criminal,' he responded in his usual stuffy nature.

'Of what crime do you speak of sir?' I asked outraged. 'Come now Carter, we all know what you do. How else has a gutter rat like you, climbed so high in society? It sickens me to see it. You have no place here sir,' he said, sneering distastefully down his nose.

'Be careful Godolphin. Neither I, nor my family work for your failing mine anymore. You have no power over me whatsoever. Make another remark about my character, and I will be inclined to take offence,' I said threateningly. The men I had been dealing with looked uncomfortable, and one had the good sense to steer me away from the confrontational Francis Godolphin, who looked like he was stinking drunk.

'Come Mr Carter, you have been keeping me from meeting your enchanting wife,' the man from Gloucestershire said, leading me in the direction of Marie.

'I would keep your distance from him Mr Carter. He has been bad mouthing you all night, and he's known to quarrel.

We agreed to meet the following week to go over the details of distribution. I introduced Marie, and he, like most gentlemen at the Ball, was spellbound by her beauty. The music that played was far better than the lads playing their fiddles back in the taverns. It was not long before Marie and I both braved our newly acquired dancing skills. John and Isabelle Tonkin were with us and looked on approvingly. I did not step on Marie's feet once. She was having the time of her life until Francis Godolphin attempted to ruin our night for good.

He walked into us with a full glass of claret, making no attempt to avoid our twirling bodies at all. His crystal glass was intentionally poured over Marie and me, ruining her new dress in the process. I pushed him hard, finally unable to hold my temper in check. He had not been expecting my sudden anger, and in his drunkenness, he landed hard on his backside, sliding across the marble floor like a duck on ice.

'How dare you sir!' he shouted, getting to his feet clumsily. Lord Arundell and John Tonkin were at hand in an instant, coming between the two of us to stop any violence. The music stopped, and all eyes were on us. That had probably been Francis Godolphin's intention all along.

'You are no gentleman sir; but I will teach you a lesson as a gentleman,' he threatened, taking a glove from his pocket to strike me around the face. He would have challenged me to a duel, thinking himself superior to me at the martial arts. But Lord Arundell could see what was going to happen just as I could and intervened diplomatically.

'Now gentlemen, I am sure this is just a complete misunderstanding. You will not however ruin my day with your quarrel. Instead, perhaps you can both give my guests some sport, and settle your grievances in a contest of swords. Practice swords mind you,' he added quickly.

'I apologise my Lord. I should not have lost my temper,' I said to Lord Arundell sincerely. I could see he was trying to defuse the situation, and I played my part, not wanting Marie to see any further confrontation. Francis Godolphin was not in any such mood to let the matter lie. 'I would prefer pistols sir,' he said airily. 'But I can see that you protect this wretch from harm my Lord. I will teach him a lesson I suppose with a practice sword. That is if he is not too frightened to pick one up and be humiliated in front of your guests. His father was the same you see; cowards the lot of em.'

The other guests were no different from the men and woman back in a village tavern, when a spot of bother was occurring. They loved a good bit of sport, just as much as the next man. It was unseemly for such an occasion, but now that a death match was averted, the people gathered became excited about the prospect of a duel of swords. I could not refuse after the comment about my father.

'As you wish sir,' I said simply.

In the background, ladies and gentlemen took wagers on the outcome. All but John Tonkin bet against me, knowing that Francis Godolphin had some skill with a blade. I was unknown to most of them and would have been deemed to lack the finesse needed to wield the rapier practice blades presented to us by our host.

I took up the blunted weapon and swung it around in a show to reinforce a belief of my lack of skill. In truth I was quite an accomplished swordsman. I had spent hours and hours with my friend William Vingoe, who had instructed me in the art of fencing. I had practiced his teachings relentlessly and put that skill to good use for real on my travels.

But I would play the oaf, and lull Francis into a false sense of invincibility. He did not even bother to warm up his arm. He was feeling too confident and believed he would thrash me.

A circle formed around us, and we stood on guard. The eyes of the guests were positively beaming with joy at the unexpected piece of entertainment. Marie should have been concerned for what was happening. She had thought the night was going to be like something from a fairy tale, and now I would have to fight the monster in the story. She did not worry too much. She knew my worth and had been insulted by the swine before me.

'I will try and prolong your humiliation as long as possible Carter,' he said, as he scraped the steel of his sword down my own to begin the contest.

He leaned back into a fighting stance and then thrust the blunted tip at me quicker than a viper. I parried the strike just in time, but it was never intended to hit me. He did not want the contest over that quickly after all.

I came back at him with a cut and thrust of my own, which he turned aside with the ease of someone who was comfortable with a sword in hand. But his style of fighting was nothing like the desperate kind I had experienced at sea, where a mistimed judgment could mean your certain death.

Our swords danced for dominance, but I felt sure that I could have ended the fight at any time. All the hours I had spent disciplining and honing my skill, were now bearing fruit. He didn't know it yet, but he was soon about to lose.

He stabbed his blade at my chest once again, but the strike had been obvious, and I decided that the time had come to end him and show the foul man what a miner's son could do.

I spun as I turned his thrust away, coming face to face with him in the process. I could smell the wine on his breath, but did not care, for the contest was over.

I had my blade at his exposed back and resisted the temptation to dig the weapon in hard. His shocked eyes spoke all the outrage he felt but could not utter. I held him with my other hand and gently applied pressure. He completely lost his temper then, and violently turned to elbow me in the face. But he was drunk and clumsy.

I, on the other hand was in my element and swept his leg as he came around, turning his aggression to my favour.

He hit the floor hard once again. 'Oh, I do apologise sir, you must have fallen over,' I said smiling. The crowed had no doubt lost good money betting against me, but none seemed to care as they applauded my unlikely victory. John Tonkin winked at me, but the fight in Francis Godolphin was far from over.

'Pistols damn you. I demand satisfaction you scum,' he spat hatefully at me.

'Steady on Francis,' one of the spectators chirped, as Godolphin looked around furiously for someone to hand him a gun. I had no doubt that I would have won that contest too after Samuel The Poacher's tutelage. But In the end, it was Lord Arundell who intervened on my behalf.

'Mr Cater has acted as a gentleman sir; you would do well to do the same. Go home and sleep it off Francis. You have successfully ruined a perfectly good Ball man,' Lord Arundell said dismissively.

'He is no gentleman!' he hissed. 'He is a peasant; his wife is a peasant and his family are peasants. He should be the one to leave my Lord!' I had made a fool out of him. I would regret it, just as I had the last time I humiliated him many years before. But what choice did I have? He was on a mission that night to quarrel with me.

'John Carter sir, is a dear friend of mine. I will not stand your presence any longer than necessary. Please leave now or I will set the damn hounds on you,' Lord Arundell said sternly. It was the first time I had seen him angry. Francis Godolphin could see at last, even though he was drunk that any further attempt at disrupting the evening was futile. He turned in a temper and picked up a glass of wine as he walked out cursing. We all heard a glass smashed were he had tossed it outside, before departing.

The ladies and gentlemen at the Ball were silent at first. Then they began to mutter and whisper excitedly, until suddenly they all laughed as one. I had thought that I had ruined the Arundell Ball; but I had indeed been the entertainment after all.

'Well done John; I knew you were a safe bet,' John Tonkin said in congratulation to me. 'I should leave also sir,' I replied in shame at causing such a stir on that fine occasion. 'Nonsense Mr Carter. You have given my guests a fine show; a fine show indeed. Come man, relax and enjoy your victory,' Lord Arundell exclaimed, looking like a proud father who had watched his son win for the first time. He really was like a father figure I suppose. He was certainly someone I looked up to, and a man who looked out for me. I was not ignorant to the fact that his grace went hand in hand with the money I was making him. But never the less, he treated me very well for it.

'You poor girl, let us get you upstairs and into something that's not covered in wine… Alice dear; take Mrs Carter with my daughter and see if you can find a suitable dress for her,' her ladyship told her servant, who attended to Marie kindly. Marie still looked a sight for sore eyes, even with the claret stain on her yellow dress. The Arundell's daughter chuckled and took Marie by the hand and rushed away to change into something more decent. While they were gone, I was congratulated further by all of the guests. I had indeed become the main attraction, and I did not waste the opportunity one bit. I made many friends that night, one being a very interesting young man, slightly younger than me. He had acquired land a short walk from Prussia Cove, which made us neighbours in a way. I had seen him many times before and would often watch him from a sloop and think he was mad.

His name was John Stackhouse, and he was an enthusiastic botanist.

He had been studying at Exeter University, but loved his home county in Cornwall, and returned as much as possible. He would name his own cove near mine one day. Stackhouse Cove as it would be called was a place he studied seaweed and algae. It was never a subject of interest to me, but I held on to his every word when he described his findings. He made it sound like the most marvellous thing in the world, and perhaps it was.

He was a likable fellow and was going to build a castle above his cove, a fact that made me jealous in a childish way. I was the King of Prussia Cove, but my big house would be dwarfed by his mighty piece of architecture. It was impossible not to get on with him though, and I often helped him with the construction of his new castle, as well as helping him with his love of tea.

'I say, you gave old Godolphin a proper thrashing Mr Carter,' he said impressed at my swordsmanship. 'You will have to come over and teach me one day.'

'It would be a pleasure Mr Stackhouse. How are your studies going at Exeter?' I asked him interested. 'Not as exciting as being back at home. But I enjoy my studies.'

The music had started to play again, and everyone began to look at the staircase where Marie was walking down majestically. Lord and Lady Arundell's daughter stood back to let my girl take centre stage. She never failed to amaze me.

She had changed into a white laced dress, which flowed out wide at the bottom, gently touching the stairs. She appeared to be floating down like a cloud, and not for the first time, I stood in stunned amazement.

I could tell she was enjoying the attention, and she smiled coyly and walked to my side. I was lost for words and just spun her into a waltz that seemed to last for a perfect eternity.

The night did end eventually though, and we said our farewells and apologised to our hosts again for the earlier excitement.

'No need to apologise John,' he told me informally. 'I cannot remember a more enjoyable evening. I trust you have made some new friends, as well as an enemy tonight,' he added, knowing I had been making deals with his friends all night.

'The Godolphin's and I will always be at odds my lord. It's in their nature to act like they do. But you are correct. We have made good contacts this night. Your friend from Gloucestershire will be collecting a shipment of tea and spirits at Porthleven. All the arrangements are made,' I said happy with myself. 'I will be bringing you a very large purse from the strength of your wonderful Ball my Lord. Thank you for inviting me.'

'I look forward to receiving it,' he said, rubbing his hands in a gesture of mocking greed. We laughed, and he shook my hand. 'You really do astonish me John Carter.' He turned to Marie. 'How does the dress fit my dear?'

'It is most comfortable my Lord. I would've been lost without your aid,' she replied gratefully. 'I will have John bring it back to you in the morning,' she added.

'Don't be silly Mrs Carter. Lady Arundell has already told me that she wishes for you to keep it. The least I can do for you and your outstanding husband.'

She blushed and curtsied. She was embarrassed to receive such an extravagant gift, but I wanted her to get used to the life of luxury. I would make sure she had all that she dreamed of and more, and our children would inherit it all.

Chapter 29

That night I lay with Marie under the stars, and we were fortunate enough to see one shoot across the sky. We both made a wish, and kept it to ourselves, lest they not come true. I was young and foolish then and had wished for wealth and prosperity. Marie would have wished for good health and happiness or something caring like that. One of us would get their wish.

After the Ball, we returned to the Cove and back to reality. I had made several deals that needed to be honoured. The Cove Boys conveyed messages to and from my sloops and cutters, and we went to work to arrange the logistics. I had ensured delivery of the contraband, and nothing would stop me from doing so.

'John; we have a problem,' my brother Charles shouted from outside the house a few days after the Ball. It was early in the morning, but the lads had been working for several hours already. I liked them to make use of every moment and we were all busy at the cove. My other brother Harry was standing next to him, out of breath from running up to the big house at the top of the cliff.

'Hello lad,' I said to him affectionately. 'Have you been up to no good?'

He was twelve then and was working for me at the cove ferrying messages up and down the coastline in a small dingy. He usually had someone experienced with him. Not just for his safety, but also to teach him all he needed to know about the sea and navigation. I was grooming him for greatness and wanted him to captain the many ships I was planning on having built. He had my great character and was liked by most men that he met.

Even when he got into trouble, which was often throughout his life, it was hard to be cross with him. I remember catching him drunk when he was no more than ten years old. Instead of crying for forgiveness, he started singing, until in the end I started to chuckle and forget his actions for his cheek. He had the same effect on mother too. He knew he was special, but never took liberties. The work he did for me however, he took seriously, and standing before me with the dire news, joking around was the last thing on his mind.

'Go on Harry, tell John what you saw,' Charles prompted encouragingly.

'Your cargo at Pothleven has been seized by the customs men John,' young Harry announced. He was only a lad, but I trusted his judgment over some grown men I knew. During that time, he led a group of lads his own age, and strutted around the cove and villages calling himself the Black Prince, because he believed that he was the mightiest of the Carter Brothers with the exception of me of course. I was nicknamed King Fredrick after all.

'Slow down Harry; what did you see exactly,' I asked calmly. 'Men in uniform stormed the ship last night. The Ferret was with em. They took the cargo by boat back to Penzance.'

'How do you know that lad?' I asked.

'I followed them back to harbour,' he said looking worried that I would tell him off. 'You went alone?' He nodded sullenly, expecting a reprimand. 'Good lad,' I said to him and gave him a playful jab. He visibly preened whenever I praised him. 'Did you see where they took the cargo?' I asked.

'Yes. it's in the Customs House lock up. I watched them unload it all.'

'You've done well Harry,' I told him genuinely. 'Very well.' He had acted independently and risked being taken by the duty men in order to follow the contraband. 'I will not forget it.' I would reward the little bugger for it, but before that, I had to think of a way out of my dilemma.

I was seething that one of my vessels had been taken so easily by the dim-witted duty men. Someone must have talked, and I thought about who had betrayed me, until I realised that foolishly, it had been me who had blabbed. It was me who had been the dimwit.

I had not been very discrete at the Ball. In fact, I had used the event to make deals with gentlemen, boasting about how much cargo I could bring into the country. I also mentioned, like an idiot, that I had a cargo at Porthleven. I had promised that Cargo to Lord Arundell's friend from Gloucestershire. I did not think he had informed on me. He was vouched for by John Tonkin and the Arundell's.

I did however remember that Francis Godolphin was behind me during my conversation. He must have heard it all. I had no doubt it was him, after Harry had said that Arthur the Ferret Ferris was among the men who had seized my cargo.

'Charles, we have to get it back. We have to get it all back!' I said in a temper. I had a duty to deliver those goods. If I failed in that delivery, then my reputation as the King of Smugglers would be in tatters. I was a man of honour, and a man of my word. If I told someone I would do something, then I would do just as I said. A man is nothing without his good name and reputation.

'But how do we get it back John? It's all under lock and key,' Charles said unhelpfully. 'I will tell you what we are going to do Charles. We are going to go there tonight and take back what's ours,' I told my brother fiercely. He swallowed, anxious about the consequences if we were to get caught. 'I can pick the lock John,' Harry said, eager to get involved. 'You're not coming Harry, it's too dangerous; tell him John,' Charles said to Harry, who looked distraught at the thought of being left out.

I looked at him and decided he would come. He would learn what it took to be a smuggler. Twelve years old or not, I could count on him to come with us. 'You can come with us lad,' I confirmed to him. He looked happy but tried to keep a serious face because of my foul mood that day. Charles was wise not to protest and remained silent. 'Charles, go and fetch Samuel The Poacher and round up the Cove Boys. We're going to get back our goods tonight.

In no time, I had assembled a small group, and told them what had happened and what I intended on doing about it.

'It will be dangerous, so I'm giving you all the choice to come with me, you are all free men. I would appreciate your help though,' I said at our beach gathering, and thankfully no one declined. There were ten of us in total. Any more than that would have created too much suspicion.

We sailed to Penzance, and when the sun sank into the western horizon, we waited for the dead of night, when all was quiet and peaceful. I had been operating without hindrance for so long that I was getting lazy. King George III had been crowned as the new British monarch and was not in favour of the French Indian war, which still raged on in the American Colonies. British forces were winning that war, taking Fort Niagara and winning a decisive battle at Montreal. They had essentially beaten the French in America and were pushing hard to kick them off the continent for good. The war was becoming expensive however, and revenue taxes were needed to pay the exorbitant sums necessary.

William Pitt the Elder, our Prime Minister, was carving out an Empire. He was paying the masterful strategist King Fredrick of Prussia an annual subsidy of seven hundred thousand pounds. He was in fact financing the great King to fight the French in Europe and win the war on the continent on Britain's behalf.

Subsequently the prices of goods went up from high taxation, making more profits for the smuggling man, but also more risk. The customs men were increasing, and although I had some working for me, I could not possibly afford to buy them all off. The men that had taken my goods were not for sale.

Francis Godolphin had no doubt instructed his man the Ferret to seize my property in a vengeful move to get me back for his humiliation at the Arundell Ball. I did not care who, or why he had taken it. All I knew was that I would get it back.

We rowed into harbour nervously, watching for any sign of life or watchmen. Some of the lads sipped gin to help them cope with their nerves. Arriving as quietly as possible, we made our way to the Customs House. No light guided our path, but I could just about make out Harry's thick dark locks of hair in the half moonlight. He went to work on the storeroom lock, defeating it within a minute. No one would have been inside at that time of night, but I crept around the place just to make sure.

Once satisfied that we had the place to ourselves, I dared to light an oil lamp, casting the storeroom with enough light needed to do our work, but not bright enough to draw attention from outside. The barrels of brandy and wine had been neatly stacked in lines, while our tea was being kept on top of the barrels in timber boxes.

Outside, Samuel The Poacher stood a way up the street in a decent position to act as our own watchman. He had his longbow which would silently shoot any man that threatened violence on us. I looked outside and whistled to him. He whistled back to let me know the coast was clear.

Back inside the lads were wrapping the barrels in blankets and tying rope to secure them around. This helped to soften the noise they would have made if we had not wrapped them. One by one my cargo was taken to our waiting men at the harbour, and then ferried out to our sloop. We worked for a long time before the last of my goods was loaded onto the boat. Samuel came inside the Customs House and noticed I had left all the other seized contraband which had been taken and held there from other smugglers. 'Are we not going to clear it out and take the lot John?' he whispered to me. 'No,' I breathed back to him. It's not ours. I will not steal Samuel; I only wish to take back what is mine.' I would find out later that they had guessed it was me who had broken into their store. They knew because I was known to be an honest man. My reputation for my honesty was everything and was the reason I prospered. But for what I did that night, my reputation would place me in danger.

'Come on, let's go,' I announced, realising we had taken everything that they had taken from me. It had been surprising to find no resistance that night, but looking back, the customs men had never needed to guard their storeroom overnight, so why would they go to the trouble of guarding it then. They had not counted on someone being brave or stupid enough to take back what they had seized. Young Harry replaced the lock and secured the doors once more, and we then made our departure to Porthleven where I intended to distribute the goods as soon as possible. I could show a clean hand if they came looking for it again. Inevitably of course, they most certainly would come looking.

Chapter 30

With our goods sold and our deal done I returned to the cove with the lads in triumph. I had a mind to travel up to Lord Arundell's house, but the journey to Trerice was too far. We still had contraband to move and I expected the customs men to make my life difficult. His house was near the northern coast of the county, not far from Newquay, and I sent him a message about what had happened, so he would not be at a loss when he eventually heard the news.

'Samuel has shot a fine bird for dinner my love,' Marie said as she prepared the table for our evening meal. The Cove Boys were making merry in Bessie's beer house, but I wanted to enjoy a home cooked meal with my family. Around the table sat Marie, my son Thomas, who was making a mess of the table cloth with spilt supper. The babe Elizabeth, my little princess, sat on her mother's lap, gurgling happily while we ate our delicious meal.

Even though it was summer, there was a slight chill in the air. Not an unpleasant chill mind you, but just enough to warrant the small fire I had burning, warming us all nicely.

I gazed at a portrait I had purchased of King Fredrick of Prussia and mused if he would have approved of my masterful stroke to reclaim my property. Who knew? But I had felt a moment of utter contentment at the dinner table that night.

'Sounds like you have visitors John,' Marie said in mild warning. I heard the horses approaching outside too and stood from my meal to look out of the window. An aggressive knock on my door stopped me in my tracks and Marie held Elizabeth tight, Thomas had a slight look of concern at the sudden noise.

'Open in the name of the King!' They shouted.

I had nothing hidden at the cove, expecting the arrival of the Duty men eventually. So, I opened the door with confidence, knowing they would find nothing to incriminate me.

As I opened the door, my eyes went wide in shock at seeing the end of a pistol barrel being levelled at me by Arthur The Ferret Ferris. I did not hesitate in slamming the door in his face, somehow sensing he would fire before he asked any questions. I had been correct. The explosive shot tore through the softwood door, leaving a splintered hole, narrowly missing me, as I dropped down for cover.

I jumped back up to lock the door to prevent the men outside from entry. Behind me the children screamed from the frightening commotion. Marie looked into my eyes sadly. 'Get down Marie… Thomas, lay down on the floor!' I shouted at them.

Thomas did as he was told and covered his ears terrified. Marie didn't move. She just watched me, breathing heavily. Her chest rose and fell rapidly and then it dawned on me.

I could see the tiny hole in her dress, and then watched in horror as it began to turn crimson. I cared nothing for my life in that moment and ran to her side to take Elizabeth from her loving arms. I checked the baby for any harm, and God be praised she was without injury. I placed her behind a wooden chest next to the table, and pulled Thomas's leg, sliding him behind with his sister.

'Open the door Carter!' Shouted The Ferret as he tried to break in, and finish his murderous work. I held Marie steady, not listening to the pounding boots trying to gain entry. It had strong hinges and would hold out for a while yet.

'Marie!' I shouted in a panic. I ripped her dress to look at where the shot had entered. Dark blood was pumping out of the wound, and I removed my shirt to stem its flow. Marie's face was pale, but still serene. She did not scream or cry out from the dreadful pain she must have been in. Outside, I vaguely heard shots fired, and hoped the Cove Boys had heard the shot and come to my aid.

The shirt I had covered Marie's wound in was now soaked in blood, and I was fighting to save her life. My old partner James had not stood a chance from his severe injuries. Marie in contrast had only a small hole in her chest. But it was bleeding profusely, and there was no exit wound, which meant the shot was still inside.

'It's alright my love,' I said to her welling up with tears. 'Help is coming. Hold on!' Her eyelids fluttered, and I felt her hand reach for mine. She still had enough strength to squeeze it, and she looked at me and smiled.

'I love you John Carter,' she said, and leaned in, to kiss me tenderly on my lips. I could taste the sweetness of the wine she had been drinking. Then she leaned back and let out a final breath.

Her eyes closed, and I held her, sobbing like a child, not excepting that she had truly gone. I shook her, trying to perform a miracle. 'Marie!' I screamed. 'Don't go my love.'

I must have held her for a good ten minutes before I realised there was nocking again at the door. But this time I heard the voice of her mother Bessie. In the distance there was still the odd crack of gunfire. I lay her reverently down on the slate floor and kissed her once more on her head.

My hands were shaking as I opened the door to let in her mother, who rushed in with some lads, Charles among them. She went to her daughter's body, and started screaming, demanding what had happened, as she stroked Marie's hair. My brother stood in stunned silence. He did not need to ask what had happened.

'Where are they Charles?' I asked in cold rage. I did not wipe the tears that streamed down my cheek. I could barely comprehend what had happened. But for my sins, I thirsted for revenge. I ran into a room which I had turned into a small armoury and loaded two pistols and took a hatchet I had brought back with me from the colonies. It would be butchers work for the swine that had so cruelly took my Marie from this world. I am old now, with many regrets in life. But on that day, I ran out from the big house looking for blood; with no regrets what so ever.

As I ran down the track, there were bodies lying dead here and there. They all wore the uniforms of the customs riders but none of them were The Ferret. Some had been shot with arrows, which told me Sam was on their trail. I hoped he had left Arthur Ferris alive, so I could be the one to end his miserable life.

I ran up the hill at speed and could have run forever and not have fatigued from it. My pain, gave me strength to find the foes that had attacked. I found Samuel at the top of the hill crouching for cover. He had run out of arrows to fire and was being pinned down by pistol and musket fire coming from a nest of long grass. Three men were firing and reloading. One of them was The Ferret who sneered down his sights waiting for the chance to blow Samuels head off.

But I did not care whether I lived or died and ran passed Samuel without breaking stride. I pulled the two pistols I had brought with me smoothly from my belt and pulled the firing hammers back with my thumbs, as I stormed towards the waiting guns.

They fired as one, and a musket ball seared my shoulder, but caused little harm. It was miraculous that they had not killed me at such a short range. But men are clumsy when they are scared. And I must have been a fearful sight indeed, as I came at them in silent wrath, with the still warm blood of Marie covering my naked upper body, making me appear demonic.

I levelled the pistols at the men flanking The Ferret and fired without mercy. I had aimed for their heads, and both shots punched into their marks true. They fell together leaving Arthur scrambling for his sword. He drew the heavy blade just in time. I however was in no mood for a duel, and pulled my hatchet, which I threw overarm at him with all the effort that my vengeful hate could muster. He tried to bat the small axe away and missed the speeding blade that thudded into his ribcage, breaking bone and knocking him onto his back.

I leaped at him to retrieve my weapon, but he prodded the sword he was still holding at me desperately. Whether he killed me was irrelevant, and I gripped the swords blade in a tight grip and reached down to pluck back my hatchet to finish him off.

The sword sliced through my palm and turned the blade red with my own blood. But I held tight, and pulled my hatchet clean out from his chest in a spray of blood. He squealed in pain, and I moved my shredded hand down to his swords hilt powerfully. He had lost the will to attack me, and I raised the hatchet, intent on ending him in a berserk frenzy. But some small measure of sanity stayed my hand, and I held the hatchet high, ready to bring it down upon him.

'You will hang for this Carter!' he spat vehemently. 'You have attacked the Kings men,' he added.

'You've killed my wife Arther. I don't give a damn if I swing. I will meet you in hell eh?' There was fear in his face when I said that. He was the one who had fired into my home after all. He was the man who had killed her.

Gradually he realised that he was in a fight for his life and wouldn't be shown any quarter. He did not guess that I had hesitated in landing the blow because of pity. He must have assumed I was just savouring the moment.

'You will go to hell first Carter!' he cried and pulled a dagger to place in my guts. He would have done too, but as he pulled the blade free I buried my hatchet into his chest with all my sadness and anger behind it. The strike was so hard; the head of the hatchet buried itself inside his chest cavity, killing him near instantly. It was a death too quick for what he had done. But it was over.

I felt a hand rest on my shoulder and turned to see Samuel looking stricken. He had heard me shout of Marie's fate. He believed the truth of my words when he saw the sorry state I was in.

'I am so sorry John,' he said to me emotionally. I had never seen him cry in my life. He was too hard to comprehend the emotion.

But seeing my grief had broken him, and we walked back to the big house together in tears. 'What shall we do with the bodies?' He asked before I went back inside. He would not enter knowing who lay dead within. Not unless I asked him. 'Get the lads and bury them at sea. Tie something heavy to them so they stay buried eh Sam,' I told him, numb from what had happened.

Chapter 31

They searched for the missing men, but they were never found of course. Fortunately, they had not told anybody that they had come to Prussia Cove. My lads had stayed tight lipped about the whole affair also.

I only speak of it now because I am too old to care of the consequences.

We buried Marie in the Garden at the big house overlooking the sea. All my large family attended that sad day, as did all of my friends and acquaintances. The cove had never seen so many people.

Bessie, like me, took it badly. She had been quarrelsome with anyone who tried to console her, so people left her well alone. I sought comfort from a different companion; drink.

I think I spent a good few months blind drunk or unconscious from its consumption. It was my little brother Harry that eventually tried to snap me out of my melancholy.

'Are you going to take care of your children John, or are you just going to mope around all day?' he said without remorse.

The King of Prussia Cove

'Are you the head of the family now then Harry?' I answered his question with a question of my own. He shook his head, and placed his hands on his hips, looking much older than his twelve years.

'I might as well be brother, but this is all yours. You built it for your family. I'm sure Marie wouldn't want you to just wallow in your own misery,' he said with passion.

I knew he was right, but I could not escape my grief. I had thought about joining the navy with William Vingoe; anything to lose myself somehow. Eventually my mother proved the voice of reason.

She came to the house one rainy day and threw a bucket of cold sea water over me as I lay drunk and covered in vomit.

'Go away!' I shouted, but she just fetched another bucket, then another, until I sobered up.

'You have suffered a terrible loss my son that is true. But you are a Carter, and I won't see you ruin your life. Now stand from your pit and clean this place up,' she ordered.

I had needed her tough love at the time, which she gave to me in spades. She stayed with me for a few more months until one day I felt strong enough to resume my business.

Charles and young Harry had once again proved themselves to be invaluable and met every delivery I had taken from my regular customers.

But before I could return properly, I had another unexpected visitor at my door.

When I opened it, I had expected to see one of the lads with some kind of problem. I could not have been more wrong. For standing before me was none other than Lord Arundell himself.

We had spoken at Marie's funeral briefly, but on that day, I had not been the best conversationalist.

'How are you John?' he asked sympathetically

'I've been better sir, I must declare.' I offered him some cake and tea, which he accepted readily. After some brief small talk of business and politics, we took a stroll along the cliffs.

'Let me cut to the chase John; I want to do you a service,' he said kindly.

'What service could you perform for me?' I asked, and he reached into his jacket pulling out a neatly folded piece of paper with a broken wax seal.

'For all the money you have made me and the other investors, I thank you. I have taken the liberty to enquire on a school place for your son Thomas. It must be hard to take care of them considering the circumstances.'

I was teaching the boy his letters and numbers when I could, but I did not want him to have the life I had. I wanted him to be among the elite, and Lord Arundell had most generously made that dream come true.

'It's Westminster School in London; fully funded by me of course. I will not hear any protests from you about that Mr Carter.'

'I don't know what to say sir,' I said stunned at his gesture. 'How can I repay you for it?' I added.

'By coming back to us man. You have lost your way recently, and I am here to help you back. We will care for your daughter Elizabeth if you wish, and make her a proper lady eh,' he said in good humour. I knew he wanted me back to keep the money flowing as it always had been. But I was still grateful for the offer, which I accepted.

'Thank you, sir, if ever I can do you a service in the future, you need only ask.'

I know Carter, I know. I may very well do that one day.

THE END

If you enjoyed this book, I would be most grateful if you could leave a review on Amazon. I love to read feedback from readers, and reviews really make a difference to an author's success.

Thank you for reading The King of Prussia Cove, Smugglers of Cornwall.

Find out about other works by John K Martin including books coming soon at: www.johnkmartin.weebly.com

***

Historical Note

Although a complete work of fiction, some of the people, places and events are largely based on fact, or legend.
Most of my sources were gained from the biography written by John Carters younger brother- Harry Carter. I must say that the book was hard to read in places, but overall enjoyable.

Harry's larger than life character bled through his writing, and I have attempted to influence John Carter's persona in the same fashion.
The part where John steals his cargo back from Customs House is true, as was his parent's and members of his family. William Vingoe was indeed a captain on the naval vessel, The Wolf and was reputed to be involved with smuggling and wrecking activities with the rest of the Vingoe family. I have however used poetic licence to bring these characters together, as I have with many other characters in the book.

The King of Prussia Cove

Lord Arundell, the Borlace family and the Tonkin Family are also based on real characters, as were their agents. John Tonkin for example was in fact Mayor of Penzance, and in 1770 was removed from the office for being involved in smuggling activities. I have tried to keep the book as accurate as possible, but for the sake of where I wanted the story to go, I placed my characters in countries and locations which they may well not have visited.
John Carters voyage to America and Jamaica for instance was something I wished to include, to highlight the effects of the French Indian war on the Colonies at the time. I also wanted him to witness the horrors of slavery, and brought him together with John Pinney, who was a real sugar merchant. His sexual orientation is again fabricated by me to highlight the most certain homophobia at the time.

His encounter with the slave Prince Hall did not happen, but Prince Hall was real, and worked in a leather store in Boston.

Prussia Cove; or Porthlegh, is a real place where the Carter family carried out their smuggling operations, until the coastguard built cottages there in 1825 so they could stop the trade at its source.

Bessie's Cove runs side by side with Prussia Cove, and Bessie did indeed have a beer house at the top of the cliff edge.

There was also a large house built overlooking the cove but was demolished in the early twentieth century. A photograph of the house was taken before hand though, showing its imposing location.

The Carter Family were well known Methodists and John Wesley was a famous preacher of the movement in Cornwall at the time. As well as Wesley, I have tried to include as many real people, legends and stories as possible.

John K Martin

I found out about William Blyth while at the Punch Bowel in Paglesham in Essex, where I discovered tales of his activities around the South East of England, as well as sampling some of the fine ales on tap there.

I would like to acknowledge the following sources which helped to write this story: Cornish Wrecking 1700-1860, Reality and Popular Myth by Cathryn Pearce.
Smuggling in the British Isles by Richard Platt. And of course, I must include Harry Carters own account of events, in his book – The Autobiography of a Cornish Smuggler.
www.smuggling.co.uk also proved to be brimming with interesting stories which helped the book no end.

The book finishes while John Carter is still a reasonably young man. But this is not the end of his story. Perhaps the King of Prussia Cove and little Harry have more adventures yet to tell.

OTHER BOOKS BY JOHN K MARTIN

Escape From Redeem - Rise of an Emperor

Mind Shift, Poetry of Love and Loss

The Librarian, A Billionaire Romance

***

Printed in Great Britain
by Amazon